INFLUENCER MARKETING FOR BRANDS

WHAT YOUTUBE AND INSTAGRAM CAN TEACH YOU ABOUT THE FUTURE OF DIGITAL ADVERTISING

Aron Levin

Apress®

Influencer Marketing for Brands: What YouTube and Instagram Can Teach You About the Future of Digital Advertising

Aron Levin
Stockholm, Stockholms Län, Sweden

ISBN-13 (pbk): 978-1-4842-5502-5   ISBN-13 (electronic): 978-1-4842-5503-2
https://doi.org/10.1007/978-1-4842-5503-2

Copyright © 2020 by Aron Levin

Managing Director, Apress Media LLC: Welmoed Spahr
Acquisitions Editor: Shiva Ramachandran
Development Editor: Rita Fernando
Coordinating Editor: Rita Fernando

Cover designed by eStudioCalamar

Distributed to the book trade worldwide by Springer Science+Business Media New York, 233 Spring Street, 6th Floor, New York, NY 10013. Phone 1-800-SPRINGER, fax (201) 348-4505, e-mail orders-ny@springer-sbm.com, or visit www.springeronline.com. Apress Media, LLC is a California LLC and the sole member (owner) is Springer Science + Business Media Finance Inc (SSBM Finance Inc). SSBM Finance Inc is a **Delaware** corporation.

For information on translations, please e-mail rights@apress.com, or visit http://www.apress.com/rights-permissions.

Apress titles may be purchased in bulk for academic, corporate, or promotional use. eBook versions and licenses are also available for most titles. For more information, reference our Print and eBook Bulk Sales web page at http://www.apress.com/bulk-sales.

Any source code or other supplementary material referenced by the author in this book is available to readers on GitHub via the book's product page, located at www.apress.com/9781484255025. For more detailed information, please visit http://www.apress.com/source-code.

Printed on acid-free paper

To the creators that are changing the way that we look at the world.

And to anyone that has ever been told that they are a little bit different.

Contents

About the Author vii

Introduction ix

Chapter 1:   Origins. 1

Chapter 2:   People Are Media Companies. 7

Chapter 3:   Influence Is an Outcome, Not a Profession. 19

Chapter 4:   The Art and Science of Creativity 47

Chapter 5:   Creator-Centric Strategies 79

Chapter 6:   1:1 Relationships at Scale. 95

Chapter 7:   The Four-Step Influencer Marketing Framework 119

Chapter 8:   Measuring What Matters 139

Glossary. 149

Index. 159

About the Author

With a passion for technology, marketing, and sales, **Aron Levin** co-founded Relatable to empower millions of content creators from all over the world. Clients include large consumer brands like Adobe, Google, Volvo, Ralph Lauren, Chiquita, and Heineken, but also brave direct-to-consumer start-ups like Lifesum, bioClarity, and MVMT Watches.

Aron is also known for his background at King Digital Entertainment (maker of Candy Crush and 100+ other games) where he led Advertising Operations and his role as Director, Growth at music-streaming service Spotify. He spends his time in Los Angeles, California, and Stockholm, Sweden, with his wife and two kids. He is also the author of *The Content Marketing Calendar* and the Relatable "Inner Circle" Newsletter that is published weekly to 100,000+ marketing professionals.

Introduction

Is influencer marketing dead? Effective? Worth it? Ethical? Sustainable? Content marketing? Paid media? PR? An overhyped fad? Better than digital ads?

The *autocomplete* feature from the most popular search engine in the world, with its corporate mission *"to organize the world's information...,"*[1] offers a fascinating glimpse into what questions the world is asking about any topic, at any given time. These search suggestions, or predictions (in the beginning of this paragraph), made me think about the intricacies of the influencer marketing industry.

So many questions and so many different answers. There's *no question*, however, that we live in a world where everything is getting more complex, where it's impossible to keep up with all the information that is available at your fingertips—and knowledge alone just doesn't cut it anymore. What we really need is synthesized wisdom, not additional information overload.

If you work with marketing (either for a brand or an agency), you're probably reading this book because you believe that influencer marketing can play an important, perhaps even critical, role in your business. There's a great chance that you're a marketing professional, founder, or social media creator that has seen the rise of influencer marketing and how this new digital media landscape has transformed entire industries.

Savvy marketing teams at direct-to-consumer brands like Revolve, Gymshark, and Vanity Planet have played this transition to their advantage and spun up hundreds of millions of dollars in revenue by riding the influencer marketing wave. Art exhibitions (or *museums*, if you can call them that) like Color Factory, Museum of Ice Cream, and Egg House sell hundreds of thousands of tickets in days,[2] and there's a 6-month waitlist to have your picture taken with a backdrop of giant cherries and marshmallow clouds. Even traditional brands like Adobe, Volvo, and Samsung are rapidly catching on to reconsider the distribution of their media mix to win their next generation of consumers.

---

[1]https://about.google/
[2]www.wired.com/story/selfie-factories-instagram-museum/

While these companies, and many others, have certainly transformed entire industries and changed the way we think about marketing, their impeccable timing should not be mistaken for luck. They've had to overcome the same obstacles and challenges as everybody else, asking the very same questions that lead you to where you are at this very moment.

With this in mind, my goal over the next eight chapters is to deconstruct what makes influencer marketing really work, take you behind the scenes, and show you the precise methodology, structure, and strategies that have proven to be effective across thousands of collaborations between creators and brands—from start-ups with a handful of employees to the largest brands in the world.

10,000 hours of practice

Personally, I've always valued advice from those that practice what they preach. In that regard, it's noteworthy that everything you read and all the tactics to go along are based on firsthand experience. My company, Relatable, has done over 10,000 influencer marketing collaborations (reaching well over half a billion people), across 40 different countries, in every vertical[3] that you can imagine.

Some of these insights are things that other agencies and industry experts probably would want to keep away from you. Proprietary tools of the trade, so to speak. It's not standard operating procedure to document everything you know only to give it away. Especially not if you believe that part of *your own* business offering is built on having access to that knowledge. I've even been accused of giving *too much* away, insinuating that it could lead to less business, instead of more. Obviously, I believe the very opposite to be true. Adding to this, there are lots of talks these days about the importance of transparency. Unfortunately, it's not practiced as frequently as it's preached. Instead, it's more common for brands to suffer from overpromise and industry jargon from partners that aren't educating them enough.

In times like these, the right thing to do is to share what you know that can hopefully be of value to others, with the intent of helping as many people as possible. And that's why you'll get nothing but full, radical transparency from here moving forward. These days, you win by sharing what you know with the world—not by keeping secrets. It'll accelerate the growth of our industry and help both creators and brands.

---

[3] If you've ever thought that influencer marketing was limited to fashion or beauty brands, you'll soon discover how deep the rabbit hole truly goes.

A blessing in disguise

The first iteration of *Influencer Marketing for Brands* (since then rewritten from scratch) was self-published and for sale on my company's website without any middlemen. I had full control over distribution, and it gave me unrestricted access to speak with every single book buyer, since I had their contact details.

This wasn't a strategic decision per se, but rather the consequence of not having a publishing deal in the first place. Strategic or not, it gave me an unparalleled opportunity to run my own research and speak with the many marketing teams that claimed a copy of the book, to understand exactly what kind of questions they had and the problems they were looking to solve.

Over time, no less than 5,000 marketing professionals actually helped shape the content of *this book*. Without their help, there'd be no way to know that 40% of readers struggle to identify creators and influencers that are aligned with their brand, that there's a greater chance than not (55%) that your manager is giving you a hard time about evaluating how effective your influencer marketing campaigns are, that it is very likely (76%, but who's counting!) that you're operating your influencer marketing campaigns manually, without any tools. I know that influencer marketing fraud, brand safety, and a disconnect between marketing objectives and key results all cause great concerns within your organization. See, you're not alone!

In addition to this, the research expands way beyond my own world and the experience within the company[4] that I co-founded in 2015 to insights and research that have been published by other agencies, influencer marketing platforms, industry thought-leaders, and firsthand data from the social media platforms themselves.

So, what exactly can you expect to learn?

Each chapter comes with a set of key questions and core concepts, followed by a set of field-tested frameworks, strategies, tactics, tools, and insights.

We'll begin our journey together in *Chapter 1: Origins* by traveling to the year 1730 where you'll meet the father of affordable luxury and origin of influencer marketing. A fascinating tale of the English potter and entrepreneur Josiah Wedgwood—a Steve Jobs of the 17th century.

In *Chapter 2: People Are Media Companies*, we're back to present time, where we'll take a look at the state of the advertising industry, decentralization of attention, and how people became media companies.

---

[4]www.relatable.me

Then, in *Chapter 3: Influence Is an Outcome, Not a Profession*, we'll dissect the real and often misunderstood implication of influence. We'll break down the three key levers of influence; you'll learn how to find the right influencers and creators for your brand and why it's absolutely critical to own your talent pool.

It's been said that creative without strategy is art, and creative with strategy is called advertising. Personally, I'd like to believe that great advertising is part art, part science, and in *Chapter 4: The Art and Science of Creativity* you'll learn how to use a set of proven set of creative strategies for Instagram and YouTube to incorporate to build powerful campaigns. You'll learn about the seven principles of word of mouth and the secret to writing a perfect brief. It's a very practical chapter, with an equally practical, and powerful, toolbox. With many of the fundamentals in place, we dial things up a notch in *Chapter 5: Creator-Centric Strategies*. The concepts in the chapter are not necessarily more advanced, but they do offer an entirely new perspective to influencer marketing, namely, one entirely focused on what creators are looking for when collaborating with brands, rather than the other way around.

At this point, we've come far, and the many components and tactics that are essential for building out a successful influencer marketing program are beginning to fall in place. Unfortunately, it's also quite common for both brands and creators to suffer from the many constraints that arise when it's time to ramp up their campaigns. *Chapter 6: 1:1 Relationships at Scale* reveals seven powerful tactics that will reduce 80% of your overhead and eliminate the constraints that are holding you back. In *Chapter 7: The Four-Step Influencer Marketing Framework*, you'll get a step-by-step framework to transforming influencer marketing into a scalable media channel that is fully aligned with the rest of your marketing. The framework is a very powerful, especially if you're looking to compare your influencer marketing programs with other traditional advertising channels.

Finally, in *Chapter 8: Measuring What Matters*, you'll learn how to fight fraud, amplify your influencer marketing efforts with paid media, and two powerful concepts that will change the way you think about investing in digital advertising forever: The Untracked Majority and Longevity on YouTube.

To a man with a hammer, everything looks like a nail

Finally, before we move forward, there's something I'd like to address. As a marketer, you have a toolbox. One of the tools at your disposal is influencer marketing, but it's risky to pick out the tool (the channel) before you know what you're building (your marketing objective). This is a common mistake among marketing professionals. They'll decide that their goal is to run an influencer marketing program before they identify what their actual marketing objective is.

As much as I'll advocate that you turn influencer marketing into your most valuable marketing channel, there are, unfortunately, no one-size-fits-all solutions. It's easy to get carried away and reason by analogy or the proxy of others, but don't make the mistake of picking out the tool before you know what you're building.

As such, a large part of this book is structured to help you understand why, how, and when the various ways you can apply influencer marketing to your media mix are applicable and relevant *for you* and when they are not.

Perhaps you've read statements like *"There's an 11× ROI on influencer marketing," "You'll make $7.00 for every $1.00 you spend on influencers,"* or *"Influencer marketing delivers better results than any other media channel."*

Those statements and promises are absolutely true. Someone, or even a large number of brands, absolutely got those results. But are they relevant or applicable to you? They certainly *could be*, but we shouldn't immediately assume that they are until you've assessed the situation. In fact, no strategy with substantial upside is entirely risk-free. You'll likely fail a few times before you win big, even if you're best in class. That's just a part of the game!

TO THE MANY FREELANCERS, CREATORS, AND INFLUENCERS READING THIS BOOK

In October 2017, Upwork and Freelancers Union published the results of their "Freelancing in America"[5] study (conducted by independent research firm Edelman Intelligence) and found that more than 50% of all millennial workers have engaged in the economy with some kind of freelance work in the last 6 months.

If you are a designer, videographer, photographer, writer, artist, model, or the like, selling work or services by the hour, or project, rather than working for a single employer on a regular salary, you're a freelancer. If you create content for brands, on YouTube or Instagram, you're also participating in the rapidly growing global freelance economy. It's predicted that freelancers are expected to be the majority of the US workforce by 2027, based on current growth rates trajectory. In the very near future, the job title freelancer will be more popular than any other job, combined. But not only that. The study from Upwork also observed that almost half of working millennials (47%) are already freelance, a participation rate higher than any other generation.

---

[5]www.upwork.com/i/freelancing-in-america/

The bottom line: Your seemingly strange gig as a multitasking freelancing social media creator will soon be more common than getting a "real job." If you belong to this group, the contents of this book will help you get a better understanding of what happens behind the scenes when you collaborate with a brand—and what their main challenges and problems are.

You'll understand their point of view better than ever before and become more client oriented. Brands will love working with you, not only because you create the right type of content, with the right message, to the right audience but because you understand the entire process better than they've ever witnessed with anybody else.

You'll become an invaluable partner, all while staying ahead of 10 million other content creators that are competing for a slice of the billion-dollar influencer marketing pie.

Origins

The Father of Affordable Luxury and Origin of Influencer Marketing

Beautiful forms and compositions are not made by chance.

—John Ruskin

The computer, jet engine, and World Wide Web were all British inventions.

As I'm typing this on a plane, en route from the United Kingdom to the United States (also, at one point, a British colonial territory), I realize that we owe a thing or two to the Britons. The engine outside my window seat, the laptop I'm typing on, and the www:// that likely led you to discover *this book* can all be attributed to the British. Influencer marketing also has its origins in England. And it all started almost 300 years ago, in Staffordshire, England.

From changemaker to tastemaker

Born 1730 in Staffordshire, England, Josiah Wedgwood was an English potter and entrepreneur, credited with the industrialization of pottery manufacturing. Wedgwood has been described as both a magnetic and engaging individual, but also as an obsessive perfectionist. A Steve Jobs of the 17th century. He would walk his manufacturing floor with a wooden stick and smash the

© Aron Levin 2020
A. Levin, *Influencer Marketing for Brands,*
https://doi.org/10.1007/978-1-4842-5503-2_1

ware that didn't reach his rigorous quality threshold, to make sure that his workers were working to his level of perfection. By marrying art, design, and technology, Wedgwood would transition a previously rude and uncultivated craft into a global industry—and create a company that, 260 years later, employs more than 3,000 people.

But this isn't a book about ceramics manufacturing or the Industrial Revolution.[1] This is a book about modern marketing. So what could a 17th-century ceramics manufacturer possibly have to do with present-day digital marketing?

Turns out that he was, to say the least, a little bit ahead of his time.

And as such, I'd like to share the marketing strategies that Wedgwood deployed to create the world's first "affordable luxury brand" and how he wrote the very first page in the playbook of influencer marketing, more than 250 years before Instagram saw the light of day. Not unlike Steve Jobs, Josiah Wedgwood's brilliance was not only technical but equally impressive in terms of marketing—and feeling the sense of where British consumer culture was going at the time. In ways, Wedgwood is actually credited as the inventor of modern marketing. He was an entrepreneur and marketer, ahead of his time, with a deep understanding of consumerism, culture, and how to leverage the right platforms and influential individuals to both build a brand and sell his products. Josiah Wedgwood was early to spot (and ride) the wave of the 17th-century Consumer Revolution, in ways similar to how you and other readers are likely to ride the present-tense wave of social media and influencer marketing.

Throughout this book, we'll focus on the present (and future), but first, we'll travel 300 years back in time to the very roots of influencer marketing, to understand what got us to where we are today.

Contextual relevance and aspirational lifestyle

The Royal Family, Queen, and...Tea. These are things that the Brits hold in high regard. But in the 1700s, tea drinking from expensive ceramics was an act reserved for nobility, royalty, and the upper class. Josiah Wedgwood had a deep understanding of manufacturing and industrialization—but if there was something he understood better than anything else, it would be consumer marketing. His expensive ceramic goods and teacups were in much demand from the nobility, and Queen Charlotte was so impressed by his quality threshold and perfectionism that she commissioned Wedgwood to create a range of cream-colored tableware.

---

[1] Pick up a copy of *Wedgwood: The First Tycoon* by Brian Dolan if you want to go down a deep rabbit hole of 17th-century pottery manufacturing.

In *Wedgwood: The First Tycoon*, historian Brian Dolan explains:

> *Josiah had been told that The Queen was much impressed with the service he had worked on so frantically. The pieces were finished in his unique cream color, with green and gold decorations as requested, but best of all, the engine-turned cups fitted the saucers and the lid fitted the pot. As promised, it was craftsmanship fit for a queen, and Charlotte was so satisfied with her new service that she bestowed a special privilege on Josiah.*

We can't tell for sure, but the *special privilege* was very likely a suggestion by Mr. Josiah Wedgwood himself. To honor Her Majesty, Josiah offered to rename his creamware "Queen's Ware," linking its uniqueness and brilliance to the image of the Queen—in return for using her assent to gain credibility in the marketplace for fashionable goods. With the endorsement of Her Majesty, Queen Charlotte, the most influential individual during their time, Josiah had set a plan in motion that would lay the foundation of the world's very first affordable luxury brand. In a stroke of marketing genius, Josiah immediately began advertising in local newspapers announcing that "Mr. Josiah Wedgwood has had the honor of being appointed Potter to Her Majesty," promoting his new product line of Queen's Ware.

Chaos ensues in London

Shortly thereafter, Josiah opened an exclusive showroom in London where his work could be seen on display—to build additional hype by capitalizing on consumers' newfound aspiration to live like royalty.

Brian Dolan writes:

> *The showroom caused a sensation. Carriages created a roadblock on Greek Street, in Soho, and spectators crowded around to catch a glimpse of the exhibition through the storefront windows as much as to gaze at Wedgwood's aristocratic patrons, who included Queen Charlotte, the wife of King George III.*

Picture that.

It's 1774, and Wedgwood engineered the biggest product launch of his time, through the use of newspaper advertising, fame, and word of mouth. Let's fast-forward to November 5, 2015, 240 years later.

Olivier Rousteing, Creative Director of the French fashion house Balmain, sets out to collaborate with H&M to launch their *Balmain x H&M Collection* He teams up with Rihanna, Kylie Jenner, and Gigi Hadid to name a few, to build anticipation and hype on social media to their millions of followers. These are the Queen Charlotte's of our time.

His goal? To bring exclusivity to the masses.

Roadblocks are established to keep crowds in order, and thousands of consumers are lined up for the anticipated launch. When H&M finally opens up the doors to their flagship store on Regent Street in London, just a short 10-minute walk from the Wedgwood showroom on Greek Street that opened up 240 years earlier, full chaos ensues as 3,000 desperate and excited fashion fans fight to get through the doors of the flagship store.

It would seem like history does, indeed, repeat itself.

I had the privilege of speaking with the Global Chief Marketing Officer of H&M around that time, and she couldn't believe what they had just witnessed. They'd never seen anything like it. The campaign and product launch and the power of influencer marketing were, to use her own words, "almost too effective." Little did she know that an event with striking resemblance took place just a few blocks west of their London flagship store, some 240 years earlier.

The Consumer Revolution

The showroom was just the starting point.

Josiah was early to notice how the taste and preference among aristocracy had begun to trickle down through the rest of society (what would later be referred to as the Consumer Revolution) and that it was only a matter of time before the masses would eventually aspire to own the line of products that initially were reserved for the upper class.

Tea was mainly consumed by royalty and upper classes, but the middle class had begun to embrace new ideas about luxury consumption driven by aspiration and not a pure necessity. As such, the tea industry was growing exponentially in England, and Josiah understood better than anyone else that no other individual than the Queen would have more influence in the market. The masses wanted to live like aristocrats, and Wedgwood quickly gained the upper hand by associating his Queen's Ware with luxury while mass-producing affordable products to the masses. He would proceed to expand his marketing efforts and pioneer direct mail, money-back guarantees, free delivery, buy one get one free, and illustrated catalogs. When he passed away in 1795, he was one of the wealthiest people in England.

Steve Jobs married art, design, and technology to revolutionize the way we think about both consumer electronics and brand marketing. Olivier Rousteing of Balmain brought luxury to the masses with his 1.6 million followers and a merry band of social media celebrities. And savvy modern social media-driven brands understand that influencer marketing can persuade consumers to shop out of aspiration and not just necessity.

But Josiah Wedgwood accomplished all of those things, ahead of his time, a good 250 years before Kevin Systrom and Mike Kriger set out to launch their photo-app, Instagram. To say that Josiah left an important legacy and played an important role in history would be somewhat of an understatement.

His daughter, Susannah Wedgwood, later gave birth to none other than Charles Darwin. Who would have guessed that the origin of influencer marketing is quite *literally* related to the author of *The Origin of Species*?

People Are Media Companies

The state of the advertising industry, decentralization of attention and how people overtook traditional media

> *They call us gamers, influencers, internet famous, but we know something that they don't.*
>
> —Casey Neistat[1]

---

[1] www.youtube.com/watch?v=jG7dSXcfVqE

© Aron Levin 2020
A. Levin, *Influencer Marketing for Brands*,
https://doi.org/10.1007/978-1-4842-5503-2_2

Key Questions   What's the current state of the advertising industry? How is traditional advertising perceived by millennials and Generation Z (Gen Z)? Why are media dollars moving from traditional publishers to people? What is the future of the influencer marketing industry?

Core Principles   1. Media dollars follow attention. 2. Democracy decentralized attention. 3. Knowledge is a commodity. 4. Creativity is the only gatekeeper.

In 2019, the world will spend more than 700 billion dollars on advertising. What surprised me when I first heard this number was the split between digital and analog advertising. Can you guess how much of the 700 billion dollars that will be spent on digital advertising? At this point in time, I would have assumed the number to be an overwhelming majority. But the number sits at just 40%.[2] What's more is that just 10 years earlier, the number was just 10%. It's estimated to hit the 50% threshold by 2021.

Meanwhile, TV, radio, print, and magazine advertising is, to little surprise, on the decline.

Where's all that money going, you may ask?

Two-thirds[3] of digital advertising budgets will be spent on mobile advertising. Here's where it gets really interesting and at the same time really challenging, because when measuring how much time consumers spend in the mobile browser (i.e., browsing websites on their smartphones in Safari, Chrome, or their favorite browser), the number is only around 6%, just 12 minutes out of 3.5 hours. So, the money is moving from analog to digital, from desktop to mobile, but *not* to the mobile Web, because that's not where consumers are. Goodbye, programmatic display banners, homepage takeovers, and rich media formats. This form of advertising was probably never built for a mobile experience, anyway.

On top of this, half of *millennials* now block traditional ads, while 70% of Gen Z are likely to avoid them altogether.[4] Leading market research company eMarketer has published several reports on the topic, diving deeper into what's driving the rapidly growing disapproval of traditional digital advertising—and the insights should have any traditional advertiser worried about their future.

An overwhelming majority of consumers find traditional ads to be annoying, intrusive or disrupt what they're currently doing.

---

[2] Publicis Groupe's Zenith Advertising Expenditure Forecasts, December 2018
[3] Digital Ad Spending Share, by Device, eMarketer, February 2019/Total Media Ad Spending, By Media, 2016-2022, eMarketer, September 2018
[4] AdReaction: Engaging Gen X, Y and Z, Kantar Millward Brown, 2017

In a study from mid-2018, where respondents were asked what their main opinion on digital ads was, 42% of respondents said that they were *"Too aggressive in following me on every device or browser."*[5]

Around the same time, IAB UK (the industry organization for digital advertising and media owners, agencies, and brands) commissioned YouGov to conduct a study on consumer usage and attitude toward ad blocking. They asked the following question:

> Which situations would make ad blocking users in Great Britain less likely to use ad blockers?

Respondents were given multiple options, and while most claimed that *less interruptive, annoying,* and simply *less* advertising would have them reconsider their decision to block advertising on their devices, a full 81% answered *none of the above* from a list of eleven different options.

There was absolutely nothing that would persuade them to change their minds about their decision to block advertising.

Key takeaway   Media dollars (advertising) are moving to platforms (smartphones) where there's less traditional advertising inventory (mobile browser) while consumers are making matters worse (ad blockers).

Finally, as I was researching the rise of ad blockers, I found another gem too good not to share. This one's for kicks and giggles.

In a 2018 survey[6] of 103 ad agencies, publishers, and marketers in the United States conducted by Pressboard, 27.2% of respondents said they use an ad blocker. Meanwhile, according to eMarketer forecasts, the average ad blocker usage across the general population the same year was 25.2%.

I'm not surprised, but it's rather ironic.

"Eating your own dog food" is a commonly used phrase within tech companies that refers to the practice of using your own products.

In the traditional advertising industry, however, the consensus seems to be that the stuff you feed your pets with should be kept at a safe distance. Someone should send those advertising executives to the doghouse.

---

[5] N=1079, ages 18+, Janrain, "Data Privacy Consumer survey," October 10, 2018
[6] Pressboard, August 23, 2018

Canine metaphors aside, Pressboard's research further revealed that advertising professionals are more likely to rely on their friends than on ads when they decide whether or not to purchase a product. Nearly eight in ten respondents (78.6%) said that word of mouth from friends influenced their recent purchase decision.

Meteors fall to Earth all the time

66 million years ago, an asteroid the size of a mountain traveling at 64,000 kilometers per hour collided with planet Earth. We all know what happened next. I'd like to pretend that the dinosaurs looked up at the sky earlier that day only to discard the distant asteroid as yet another meteoroid space-rock moving through our solar system at a safe distance.

Or perhaps another shooting star unlikely to survive a trip through the atmosphere. Meteors do, after all, fall to Earth all the time.

But minutes later, an explosive yield estimated at more than 100 trillion tons of TNT would wipe out 80% of life on Earth—including most of those dinosaurs. The seismic event that followed would be the equivalent to every earthquake that ever happened in history, all at the same time. Those close enough to observe the giant fireball, and unfit to survive, were first to go, and only one in five would survive what scientists today reference as the final of the five big mass extinction events. When faced with an existential threat, it's easy to think that you are the exception to the rule and that things will be okay.

But look no further than Blockbuster, Kodak, RadioShack, or Toys "R" Us to see what happens when you're too slow to adapt or you think that you're an exception to the rule. When Blockbuster finally went bust, analysts said that the Internet, on-demand streaming, and consumer behavior were to blame. But those are macro trends that inevitably changed their marketing conditions—and if you are to remain and thrive as a business, you have to adapt. Resist, or even hesitate, and you'll eventually have no option but to suffer from the consequences. In the case of the iconic video rental chain, they simply couldn't pay their late penalty fees and had no option but to file for bankruptcy.

Analysts are perhaps right to blame disruptive companies like Netflix for what happened, but it's more likely that Blockbuster sent itself into a death spiral long before consumers asked to stream their movies on demand. In early 2000, Reed Hastings (the founder of Netflix) flew to Dallas to meet with Blockbuster CEO John Antioco. He proposed that Netflix would run Blockbuster's brand online in exchange for in-store promotion across its 9,000 locations. Their response? Hastings got laughed out of the room.

John Antioco and his leadership team had been made fully aware of the Asteroid, but it was quickly dismissed as yet another shooting star. Don't be a meteor-gazing dinosaur on doomsday.

A glass half full

While the advertising industry is knee-deep in trouble, it's not just doom and gloom. There's another side to the story. A 2017 study from Kantar Millward Brown found that 77% of both Generation Z (born 1996 or later) and millennials (born between 1981 and 1995) are positive to ads that show real people in real settings.[7] Both segments also had more positive attitudes toward selected types of branded digital content: tutorials, social media feeds, sponsored events, advertorial, and other types of sponsored content. The study found that Generation Z members were not as interested in ads that featured celebrities, but receptive to ads that told an interesting story (56%), with humor (72%) and great music (58%).

See, consumers, especially Generation Z and millennials (two segments that brands can't seem to figure out), actually have a really positive sentiment toward advertising that understands their point of view—and when you achieve that, you have the opportunity to win big.

In fact, when consumer insights company Toluna Group interviewed 898 consumers (for their 2019 D2C Survey[8]) that recently had purchased a product online from a direct-to-consumer brand, they found that 34.6% first discovered the brand through an ad on social media.

And finally, a full 44.7% of US Internet users between ages 18 and 34 say that they have bought a product/service recommended by an online influencer on YouTube or Instagram.[9]

In 2019, for the first time, US consumers will spend more time with their mobile devices than they do watching TV, more than 3.5 hours per day, on average.[10] And while most of Gen Z or millennials won't sit through a 30-second ad, they'll happily spend 40 minutes, on average, each time they browse YouTube on their smartphones. It's noteworthy that digital audio now accounts for the biggest share of time spent, with social media and digital video following. We listen to podcasts while browsing Instagram and Facebook or watch videos on YouTube to be entertained, learn new things, and solve problems.

---

[7] AdReaction: Engaging Gen X, Y and Z, Kantar Millward Brown, 2017
[8] Toluna, "D2C Survey," March 6, 2019
[9] Clever Real Estate, "Marketing to Millennials in 2019"
[10] "US Time Spent with Mobile" report, eMarketer, May 2019

THE IMPACT OF YOUTUBE

- Six in ten YouTube subscribers would follow advice on what to buy from their favorite creator over their favorite TV or movie personality.

- Seven in ten YouTube subscribers say that YouTube creators change or shape culture.

- 70% of teenage YouTube subscribers say they can relate to YouTube creators more than traditional celebrities.

- 86% of viewers on YouTube say they regularly turn to YouTube to learn something new.

Source: "The Values of YouTube" Study, Oct. 2017.

In July 2017, there were more than 2,000 TV channels, 1,000 newspapers, and 7,000 published magazines in the United States. Their common struggle for survival has been widely reported—and it's not *that* surprising when you couple the numbers with the growth of platforms like Instagram and YouTube. To put those numbers in perspective, there are more than 3,000 YouTube channels in the United States alone with more than 100,000 viewers per video (July 2019) and 38,500 creators on Instagram with more than 100,000 followers, a number that has increased by 400% since July 2017.[11]

The democratization of media

In 2017, filmmaker and YouTuber Parker Walbeck teamed up with smartphone maker LG to demonstrate the quality of the camera in their latest flagship model, the LG V30.

Recreating the famous longboard scene from *The Secret Life of Walter Mitty* in a YouTube video that has since racked up more than 3 million views, the entire sequence was shot—by Parker—with a smartphone from the same year, an LG V30 mounted on a $140 Smooth Q Stabilizer next to a $50,000 RED camera. The dual-camera setup (with the smartphone *literally* duct-taped to its 100x more expensive distant cousin) would allow the filmmaker to directly compare video quality from the two. A brilliant marketing campaign as it sets out to prove an important point: Unless you're a professional filmmaker, it's hard, almost impossible, to tell a difference when you look at the final footage, even when played frame by frame in split screen. You'll have to

---

[11] Relatable, internal data analysis between 2017 and 2019

see if to believe it. The video is titled *"LG V30 vs. $50,000 RED Weapon—Replicating the Walter Mitty Longboard Scene."*[12] There are thousands of comments on the video, and the consensus within the YouTube community is clear: The creative direction, and not the tools, is what creates cinematic masterpieces. The same has happened to aerial photography.

What would previously have required a custom-built helicopter, a pilot, city permits, and a specialized camera team operating expensive camera gear can now be accomplished with an off-the-shelf $1,495 DJI Mavic 2 Pro drone.

Too hefty of a price tag? How about renting one for $37 per day?

For the past 100 years, you had to possess both capital and knowledge to compete with professional filmmakers. Nowadays, the tools are accessible to everyone, and you no longer have to pay a $77,000 per year tuition to attend the USC School of Cinematic Arts. Personal growth is held back only by creativity and not by lack of access to knowledge or capital.

Just ten short years ago, traditional media still ruled Earth, dictated attention, and decided who would be famous—but you no longer need their approval.

A walk down the Walk of Fame

There are more than 2,600 brass stars embedded in the sidewalks along Hollywood Boulevard, bearing the names of musicians, actors, directors, producers, and even fictional characters. Each year, the Walk of Fame Committee selects approximately 30 names for insertion into the Walk. Kermit the Frog, Godzilla, and Donald Trump[13] all have a star! It made me wonder. Clearly, if *they* qualify, a YouTuber or two must have made the list. But no.

In an interview[14] from 2013, a spokesperson for the Walk of Fame and Hollywood Chamber of Commerce clarified that *"We don't have reality stars on the Walk of Fame. We're happy to consider reality stars once they get nominated for, or win, an Emmy, a Grammy, an Oscar. We'll consider them when they're legitimate actors or singers."*

Half a decade later, I suppose the question isn't if you deserve a star on the Walk of Fame, but to what extent your fans, followers, or subscribers would even care if you do.

Hollywood still matters, but there's a diminishing impact and the tables have turned even for the traditional entertainment industry. Dwayne "The Rock" Johnson has a separate section in his movie contracts stipulating how much

---

[12] www.youtube.com/watch?v=nAth8gO5tfs
[13] For producing Miss Universe, rather than reality show *The Apprentice*
[14] Ana Martinez, spokeswoman for the Walk and the Hollywood Chamber of Commerce in an interview with Yahoo! Entertainment on October 11, 2013

he'll get paid to promote his movies in his own social media channels—and it's in the seven-figure range. Here's what Forbes discovered, as told in a story[15] from 2018 by Natalie Robehmed:

> *In addition to hefty $20 million up-front paychecks and cuts of back-end studio profits—starting with July's Skyscraper, in which he [Dwayne Johnson] plays a former FBI hostage-rescue leader—he'll insist on a separate seven-figure social media fee with every movie in which he appears, according to people familiar with his deals. In other words, rather than have studios dump money into TV ads or billboards, their new paid-marketing channel doubles as their marquee star.*

> *"Social media has become the most critical element of marketing a movie for me," Johnson says. "I have established a social media equity with an audience around the world that there's a value in what I'm delivering to them."*

In an interview with Porter Magazine,[16] *Game of Thrones* actress Sophie Turner revealed that she landed a part over a superior actress because she "had the followers." The actress said:

> *I auditioned for a project and it was between me and another girl who is a far better actress than I am, far better, but I had the followers, so I got the job. It's not right, but it is part of the movie industry now.*

She's right, but also wrong. It's not that her influence in social media is a part of the movie industry—it's actually the other way around. Until recently, actors would appear on the red carpet for a chance to earn a front-page feature. That's how the entertainment industry leveraged the media to gain exposure. It was a highly effective way for actors to become more famous and hopefully land their next paycheck.

But nowadays, studios track social media following and engagement to make casting decisions. These days, the entertainment industry is writing a paycheck to the actor in exchange for promotion in their social media channels while the traditional media are nothing but a passive bystander.

How did this come to be?

Through access and democracy.

---

[15] "Why The Rock's Social Media Muscle Made Him Hollywood's Highest-Paid Actor," Forbes, July 13, 2018
[16] Issue 22, Fall 2017

The best time to plant a tree

There's a popular Chinese proverb that says: *"The best time to plant a tree was 20 years ago. The second best time is now."*

But why plant a tree today if you can plant a faster-growing tree for less tomorrow? That's what technology, the Internet, and social media have done to the traditional publishing world and other parts of society as well.

The tools are cheaper, there's an even bigger audience, and you can piggyback on the mistakes (and success) of others.

That's what has happened in the media industry in the last 10 years. Previously, you'd be in the hands of journalists, media moguls, or Hollywood power players to get in front of an audience.

Nowadays, you don't need the front page, a TV show, or a lead role in a feature film. It truly is a world without gatekeepers, and the only person you need permission from is yourself, and an audience. And the audience can be a very small segment of the market.

In the 2017 book *Hit Makers: How to Succeed in an Age of Distraction,* Derek Thompson dives deep into the secret histories of pop culture hits and the science of popularity. He writes:

> *A simplistic definition of "popular" is the quality of being well-liked by most people. But the trouble with this definition is that there are few things that most people like.*

He extends his reasoning to conclude that *"from a majoritarian standpoint, nothing is popular. The mainstream doesn't exist. Culture is cults, all the way down."*

This is true in book publishing, scripted movies, and social media. In June 2018, Instagram announced that it had reached an important milestone—1 billion monthly active users. It goes without saying that if you have a million followers on Instagram, you're one of the most popular users on the platform. And if you happen to be one of the 11,621 users that belong to this rare group, congratulations, you're now a part of the 0.001%.

You are one of most popular users on one of the largest social media networks in the world! But as strange as it may sound, while you may have built a larger following than 99.9% of the population, you're simultaneously ignored by 999 million people, or 99.9%. Even with an audience of a million followers, if you were to get up on a stage in a room with a thousand random strangers that are active social media users, only one in a thousand would recognize who you were. You're world famous to a million people, but they represent a minority of the entire population. The same is true if you have an audience of 100,000, 10,000 or 1,000 followers, subscribers, or fans. You are famous to them and you have their permission to express your creativity, and that's the only thing you need. When you can get your hands on a drone and learn how to operate one on YouTube, and distribute your footage for free to anyone on the planet, there's an entirely leveled playing field. Your ability to, as YouTuber Casey Neistat remarks in one of his most popular videos,[17] *"do what you can't"*—to push the boundaries of creativity and innovation—is the only thing that will truly set you apart.

Casey narrates the video: *"When I said I wanted to make movies, they said: You can't, you didn't go to film school. You can't have a talk show!"*

Then, he adds: *"But, you have a webcam… and you can! When you're a creator, all you need is a phone, an internet connection, and a good idea. A story you want to share, something you need to say, and the rest is history. And the next thing you know, you're interviewing the president."*

The latter in reference to a video from 2016, when YouTuber Liza Koshy Too interviewed Barack Obama on her YouTube channel. This is obviously raising the bar. Suddenly, creators have to step up their game. They are, after all, competing with tens of thousands of other talented creators, and that's just within their specific subcategory.

The same is true when you, as a marketer, work with a talented social media creator. If we both hire a photographer to take pictures of the same subject, with the same gear, and the same circumstances, the outcome will differ wildly depending on how we instruct (brief) for the photoshoot. The more experience you have, the better the outcome.

Just remember: Be careful not to suffocate creativity with an unintentional chokehold. Writing an effective brief that balances creativity and marketing objectives is a true art form that is covered in depth in Chapter 4: The Art and Science of Creativity.

Astronauts and pirates

With all the world's information at our fingertips (*turning knowledge into a commodity*), and Moore's Law (the principle that the speed and capability of computers can be expected to double every 2 years, as a result of increases in the number of transistors a microchip can contain) in play (*driving down costs and a reduced need for capital*), the only thing that's standing in our way is innovation (*creativity*).

On one end of the spectrum, you'll find Elon Musk. He probably couldn't have built spaceships in the 1970s, but fast-forward to 2019 and his company, SpaceX, is now head to head with NASA—a state-funded organization

---

[17] www.youtube.com/watch?v=jG7dSXcfVqE

that has spent $339 billion over the last 17 years, while SpaceX has raised just $3.2 billion.

On the other end of the spectrum, you'll find podcasts and audio broadcasts.

In 1964, when rock n' roll was still considered unfit for public broadcast, Irish businessman Ronan O'Rahilly had to operate his offshore radio station, Radio Caroline, on international water—out of British authorities' legal reach. With the exception of a commercial TV network, the airwaves were owned by the British Broadcasting Corp (BBC).

The pirates would stream music from American top 40 stations, featuring artists like The Rolling Stones, The Beatles, and The Who, and would eventually become one of the most popular radio stations in the country.

The pirate radio station was never illegal, but in 1967, the British government made it a crime to supply music, commentary, fuel, food, and water to any unlicensed offshore broadcaster, an act that, figuratively speaking, would eventually sink their pirate ship.

Nowadays, anyone can be a pirate. No need to run from the law and worry about winter storms or food supplies. Got an interesting story? Find a quiet room, decent microphone, and some free audio software, and you'll compete for attention against the largest broadcasters in the world.

We've returned to both the golden age of space exploration and piracy—and a great time to be either an astronaut or pirate.

Conclusion

The eyeballs are on other people, regardless of what social media platform they publish their content on.

A few years ago, the eyes were on Blogger, WordPress, Twitter, and Facebook. Today it's Instagram, YouTube, and Snapchat. Who knows where it will be in another few years from now or what the formats will look like, but I'd bet you that we'll consume content from other people.

Individuals have more publishing power than the largest media companies in the world had less than 20 years ago, and where the eyeballs and attention are, the advertising dollars likely will follow.

And our job, if we wish to remain in our profession as marketers and digital advertisers, will be to follow along and play by the rules of the consumer. With that said, think of digital content creators not merely as "social media stars" but as modern magazines or TV channels.

You're working with modern media publishers to advertise your message in a way that resonates with the expectations of the consumer. Remember the study from Kantar Millward Brown? These are consumers that are positive to ads that show real people in real settings (rather than celebrities) and are receptive to ads that tell an interesting story in social media, tutorials, and other types of sponsored content.

So, you'll want to shift your mindset and treat social media creators, and influencers, like media publishers and the investment like advertising spend.

Over the next couple of years, brands are set to allocate between 5 and 10 billion of their media dollars to influencer marketing. It's not a short-lived fad, but a tectonic shift in media consumption. But the phrase *influencer* is frequently misused and equally misunderstood. In the next chapter, you'll learn that *influence is an outcome, not a profession*—and the three main levers that hold the power to unlock the full potential of influencer marketing for your brand.

Influence Is an Outcome, Not a Profession

Context, adoption, levers of influence, and how to find the right creators for your brand

> *In a world of infinite choice, context—not content—is king.*
>
> —Chris Anderson[1]

Key Questions   How do I find the right influencers for my brand? What attributes should I look for when identifying the right influencers? Are influencers early adopters? What is a good engagement rate?

Core Principles   1. Influence is an outcome, not a profession. 2. Social media creators are early adopters. 3. Own your talent pool. 4. The power of the long tail. 5. Diffusion of innovations.

---

[1] *The Long Tail: Why the Future Is Selling Less of More*

© Aron Levin 2020
A. Levin, *Influencer Marketing for Brands*,
https://doi.org/10.1007/978-1-4842-5503-2_3

If you run a keyword search on Instagram, and limit your search to users with more than 10,000 followers, you'll find more than 14,000 creators on the platform with the title *"Influencer"* in their biography. But *influence* is an out-come, not a profession. Like celebrity, or guru, it's not a title that was ever meant for your business card. Why?

Because influence can't exist without context or a frame of reference. The common noun (i.e., *influencer*) is thrown around to describe an individual in social media with a large following—but misses the mark, in my opinion.

influencernoun: influencer plural noun: influencers

: one who exerts influence: a person who inspires or guides the actions of others

influence

noun: influence plural noun: influences

: the power or capacity of causing an effect in indirect or intangible ways

—Merriam-Webster[2]

You'll turn to one trusted source for advice on fashion and another for healthy cooking. The personal trainer you follow on Instagram will likely influence your decisions, but only within the context of fitness (and other closely related topics). The same is true when it comes to your family and friends. Different individuals shape our character, behavior, and decision making in different ways—authoritative experts, celebrities, and journalists alike. It's unlikely that a specific individual would exert a generic influence on your decisions. There are, however, levers you can push, pull, or move in different directions to change the outcome and strategies that you can apply to set things up to be in your favor.

The three levers of influence

Having worked on hundreds of influencer marketing campaigns, programs, and projects, I've identified three levers that you can move to impact the level of influence an individual you're working with can have, and this chapter is entirely dedicated to helping you find who those individuals are.

Using the example in the earlier section, with the personal trainer you follow on Instagram, their influence is entirely contextual. That specific individual, regardless of how large her audience is, or how engaged the audience is, can

---

[2] Merriam-Webster, s.v. "influencer," accessed October 1, 2019, www.merriam-webster. com/dictionary/influence

influence your decisions. Why? Expertise and credibility, the *first* lever of influence. The *second* lever is the strength of your relationship. The better you know each other, the more effective. We trust our friends, family, and those we have a strong relationship with. We also have different strength of relationship with those we follow or subscribe to online. The audience size of the personal trainer, and the number of people she can reach, functions as a multiplier. And that's the *third* lever of influence.

The Formula

Influence = Audience Reach x Affinity (Expertise, Credibility) x Strength of Relationship with Audience (Engagement).

1. Audience Reach is the size of the audience and who they are. Subscribers, followers, or a network of friends.

2. *Affinity (Expertise, Credibility)* is making sure that there's an affinity, a natural liking, or sympathy for your message or brand. It's equally about expertise, as defined by "knowledge in a particular field" and credibility, defined as "the quality of being trusted and believed in." We'll dive deeper into the attributes creators value when working with brands in Chapter 5: Creator-Centric Strategies.

3. *Strength of Relationship with the Audience (Engagement)* is about how close the audience is. If the relationship is weak, the audience isn't paying attention and the message will have low attention and low impact.

When you set yourself up to optimize for all three, you'll be more likely to build influencer marketing campaigns with a better outcome.

Audience size

Strategy: Audience first

Make sure that the creator you're working with has an audience that overlaps with your audience. Assure that you understand how many creators there are in a specific follower range and your market.

Key questions: *Who is our target audience? Who has an audience that can help us reach this audience? How large audience should each person we're working with have?*

One of the biggest challenges with influencer marketing is knowing that you're working with talent that has the same audience that you're aiming to reach. Without this knowledge, you can't really justify replacing your existing media dollars in channels that have these capabilities. By understanding who their followers are both individually and aggregated, you'll know that you're not just engaging an audience, but your audience. We'll cover how you do this in detail in section "Finding the right creators."

Affinity

Strategy: Talent independence

There are more than 2 million YouTube channels with 500+ subscribers. There are more than 10 million creators on Instagram with 1,000 followers. Work with a partner that can tap into this entire group of potential creators and help you find those that have an affinity for your brand, expertise, and credibility.

Key questions: *Affinity: Is there a natural liking for my brand or sympathy for the marketing message? Expertise: Is this person knowledgeable in my particular field? Credibility: Why is this person trusted or believed by their audience, and what's the "reason to believe" in the marketing message or your promise?*

Unless you operate completely independently, you're unlikely to get the right people onboard for your campaign. A multichannel network or talent agent will recommend their rooster and be limited to those that they represent, and sometimes they'll be the perfect fit for your brand, but other times not. That doesn't necessarily make them bad, but it limits their ability to help you build a talent pool proprietary to your business (we'll cover this in depth later in this chapter.)

With a talent-independent approach to identifying and onboarding the right people, we assure that we get the right people onboard every single time, without any compromise.

Strength of relationship

Strategy: Optimize for engagement

Engagement is a great proxy for how strong a relationship is. It's also a great way to objectively assess if the audience is paying attention to your message. Aim to work with creators that have an exceptional level of engagement. How do you build strategies and campaigns that yield an exceptional level of engagement? This will be covered more thoroughly in Chapter 4: The Art and Science of Creativity. For now, just keep in mind that engagement will be an important variable when you seek out to identify social media creators with influence.

Key questions: *What target engagement rate should I aim for? Is this number reasonable with the former two strategies in mind?*

The number of people that engage and interact with your campaign is more relevant than how many people you'll potentially reach. That's especially true if your overarching goal is to reach as many people as possible. Why is that? Unless they're paying attention, you're unlikely to change brand preference, consideration, and brand lift or see any kind of impact. By working only with those that have an exceptionally engaged audience, your campaign will see a more significant impact. A comprehensive engagement rate benchmark report across 15 major countries is available for free for at rlt.to/engagement-countries. Use the insights from the report to help answer the key questions outlined in this section.

Leaders and followers: Social media influencers as early adopters

In the early 1960s, communication theorist and assistant professor at Ohio University, Everett Rogers noticed that ideas, innovations, and new technologies would follow a similar pattern as they were spread in culture and society.

Rogers developed his *diffusion of innovations* theory and published his findings in his 1962 book: *Diffusion of Innovations*. In the book (now in its 5th edition) Rogers explains how, why, and at what rate new ideas and technologies are absorbed by society and how *innovations* are *diffused*[3] in a population. For many (if not *most*) marketers, the act of developing new ideas that spread widely in society or within a specific population is the very definition of our jobs. As such, there are several valuable marketing lessons uncovered in findings published by Everett Rogers.

Several of which are likely widely *adopted* (Get it?) within your own organization. Rogers proposes that adopters of any new innovation can be grouped by five different phases: innovators (2.5%), early adopters (13.5%), early majority (34%), late majority (34%), and laggards (16%), distributed mathematically as a bell curve. See Figure 3-1.

---

[3] Defined as the process or state of something spreading more widely

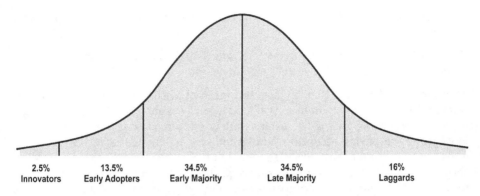

Figure 3-1. Product adoption, diffusion of innovations

Different segments have different needs, and each adopter's likelihood to accept your idea depends on understanding their unique characteristics, needs, attitudes, reasoning, and so forth. Rogers found, for instance, that *innovators* and *early adopters* will often spread the word, leading to more people accepting the idea, to a point where the idea will eventually hit a critical mass, or a point of market saturation.

The different groups, and their key traits, are described in the following way:

Innovators (2.5%)

Innovators are enthusiasts and risk takers who accept a high degree of uncertainty. They move fast and appreciate technology, innovation, new ideas, and so forth, for their own sake. They're motivated by the idea of being an agent of change and are almost obsessed with venturesomeness, driven by a desire for the rash, the daring, and the risky.

It's common for the innovator to not be respected by other members of a local system. The innovator is a gatekeeper of new ideas and thus play an important role in the adoption process.

Early adopters (13.5%)

Often the visionaries, role models, and trendsetters. This adopter category has, according to Everett Rogers, the highest degree of opinion leadership. They're "the person to check with," and it's common for others to turn to this group for advice and information about an innovation or a new idea. While innovators are driven by a desire for risk (and potentially be wrong), early adopters know that they need impeccable judgment before they put their stamp of approval on a new idea.

Early adopters often make excellent test subjects to trial a new innovation, as they're not too far ahead of the average individual in innovativeness.

Early majority (13.5%)

Members of the early majority group are more cautious than early adopters and seek to avoid risk by adapting solutions that have been proven by others. They tend to avoid complexity, and reliability is an important consideration. They pay attention to (and follow) trends, but their adoption process is more deliberate. This doesn't mean that the early majority doesn't like new products—they're not just as excited about them as the previous two groups.

Rogers concludes, through his research, those that belong to the early majority are less likely to hold positions of opinion leadership. It's easy to see why marketers and brands are obsessed with attracting the early majority: They make up a full third of your overall market and are more likely to stick with a product they like and buy it over and over again. In that sense, they differ from early adopters, who love to try things that are new.

Late majority (34%)

When marketing to this group, you're addressing the second half of your total potential market. Members of the late majority are conservative and await to adopt new ideas just after the average member of the total group. They are skeptics of innovators and early adopters and need full certainty before they feel safe enough to make a decision. Their decision-making process is slower than the previous groups, driven by necessity, cost sensitivity, and peer pressure from others in society.

Laggards (16%)

Laggards are suspicious of (and resistant to) innovation. It's a rational opinion from their point of view, as their resources are limited and they must be certain that a new idea will not fail before they can adopt. Their point of reference tends to be in the past ("We've always done things this way!"), and they tend to isolate themselves from opinion leaders.

Laggards value credibility, availability, and simplicity—and further studies have shown that there's a strong correlation between this group and both lower income and lower levels of education. Price (and awaiting price falls or promotional activities) is therefore important in their decision-making process.

This should seem familiar, basic even, because the findings have been around and been widely accepted, by most marketing professionals, for more than 50 years. Dig deeper, however, into the diffusion of innovations theory, and you'll begin to see an interesting parallel to influencer marketing. One of the big (and applicable) ideas in his book is the importance of peer-to-peer networks, and how traditional mass media is an effective way of spreading *information*, while conversations between individuals spread *adoption*. See Figure 3-2.

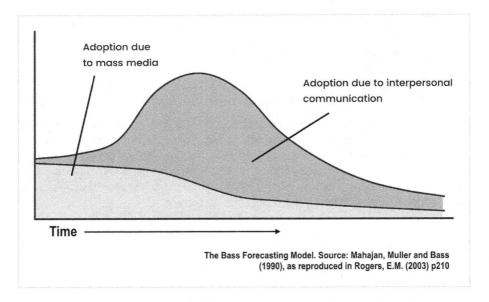

Adoption due to mass media

Adoption due to interpersonal communication

Time

The Bass Forecasting Model. Source: Mahajan, Muller and Bass (1990), as reproduced in Rogers, E.M. (2003) p210

Figure 3-2. The Bass Forecasting Model

He found:

> *While mass media channels are often the most rapid and efficient means to inform an audience of potential adopters about the existence of an innovation, interpersonal channels are more effective in persuading an individual to accept a new idea, especially if the channel links two or more individuals who are similar in socioeconomic status, education or other important ways.*

Rogers continues: *"Most people depend mainly upon a subjective evaluation of an innovation that is conveyed to them from another individual like themselves who have previously adopted the innovation."*[4]

The concept of *peer networks* is an essential element to the diffusion of innovations theory and also explains why, and how, influencer marketing is so effective. Innovators, and early adopters, effectively become opinion leaders (or *individuals with influence*) that ignite an initial "take off" adoption process, furthering the adoption of an idea to achieve critical mass.

---

[4] Everett M. Rogers, *Diffusion of Innovations*, 5th Edition (Free Press, 2003)

So, how do you identify key opinion leaders relevant to your marketing objective? Rogers suggests that there are, generally, seven key traits that set opinion leaders apart:

1. Opinion leaders have greater exposure to mass media than their followers.

2. Opinion leaders are more "cosmopolite" than their followers. They are "people on the edge" and can bring new ideas from outside their social group to its members.

3. Opinion leaders have greater contact with change agents than their followers.

4. Opinion leaders have greater social participation than their followers.

5. Opinion leaders have higher socioeconomic status than their followers.

6. Opinion leaders are more innovative than their followers.

7. Opinion leaders are more innovative when a social system's norms favor change, but when the system's norms do not favor change, opinion leaders are not especially innovative.

WHAT IS A "CHANGE AGENT"?

A change agent is an individual who influences clients' innovation-decisions in a direction deemed desirable by a change agency. A change agent usually seeks to secure the adoption of new ideas, but he or she may also attempt to slow the diffusion process and prevent the adoption of certain innovations with undesirable effects.

—*Diffusion of Innovations*, 5th Edition (2003)

Consider how these traits are related to influencer marketing and identifying the right creators, social media influencers, and ambassadors for your brand or marketing message, but be careful not to mistake innovators for opinion leaders. Opinion leaders have followers, whereas innovators are the very first to adopt new ideas and are often perceived as deviants from the norm.

Diffusion of innovations among social media influencers

If the definition of an *individual with influence* is *one who exerts influence or inspire the action of others*, you can't help but wonder if influential social media creators are more likely to be early adopters and opinion leaders. As previously outlined, early adopters are role models, trendsetters, and opinion leaders. They influence and simultaneously make great test subjects to trial what will likely be accepted by the early majority. As such, they're effectively the key to mass market adoption—to a much greater extent than any other group.

Using the key traits outlined in the *Diffusion of Innovations,* and the characteristics of the different adoption groups (innovators, early adopters, and so on), it would seem to be the case. To find out, we initiated a research project in July 2019, with more than 2,000+ participants, each a social media content creator, or *influencer* if you will, with an average of 75,000 followers on Instagram. To validate this specific thesis, survey participants were asked to answer the following question:

Compared to other people you know, how would you describe yourself?

1. *I am generally the first to try new products and services.*

2. *I am generally among the first to try new products and services.*

3. *I am generally in the middle when it comes to trying new products and services.*

4. *I am generally among the last to try new products and services.*

5. *I am generally the last to try new products and services.*

Each of the five answers corresponds to an adopter category, as follows in Table 3-1.

Table 3-1. Survey questions and adopter category

Answer	Group
1	Innovators
2	Early adopters
3	Early majority
4	Late majority
5	Laggards

If influencers are indeed early adopters, they'd be more likely to belong to the innovators and early adopters category and less likely to belong to the early majority, late majority, and laggards category. Table 3-2 shows what we found.

Table 3-2. Comparison of adoption (influencers, general population)

Group	Influencers	General Population	Difference
Innovators	29%	2.5%	+1040%
Early adopters	48%	13.5%	+255%
Early majority	21%	34%	-37%
Late majority	1%	34%	-97%
Laggards	1%	16%	-93%

The bell curve is suddenly compressed to the left, with 29% of influencers identifying as innovators and 48% identifying as early adopters (Figure 3-3). On the other side of the distribution curve, they're as much as 96% less likely (2% vs. 50%) to belong to the late majority or laggards stages.

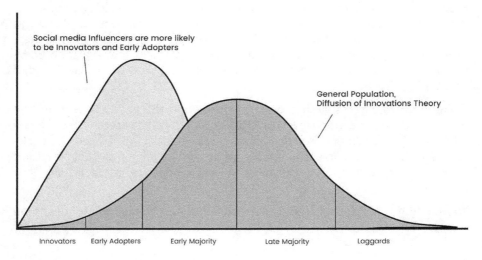

Figure 3-3. Social media influencers are more likely to be innovators and early adopters

Compared to a population average, and research that led to discovering the diffusion of innovations theory, social media influencers are on the other hand 10× more likely to be innovators and 2.5× more likely to be early adopters.

This is remarkable and suggests that influencer marketing can not only replicate the characteristics of a traditional mass media channel to spread information but also drive conversations between individuals that spread adoption.

Social media influencers are, in short, early adopters. That being so, if you believe in the *diffusion of innovations theory*, they influence the early majority to a greater extent than members of late majority or laggards. The same research project revealed a few other interesting insights as well, among other things the answer to another important question: **Who influences those with influence?**

Do you trust your doctor?

"More Doctors Smoke Camels Than Any Other Cigarette" reads an iconic (and wildly misleading) 1946 print ad that ran for a total of 8 years in the United States.

During that time, from the 1930s to the late 1950s, physicians, doctors, and models in white lab coats were frequently hired by the major tobacco companies to propose that their deadly products were *"just what the doctor ordered!"* while slapping a *"doctors recommend"* label onto their packaging.

Fortunately, Big Tobacco are no longer allowed to apply any such practices in their advertising and are both banned from certain advertising tactics and heavily regulated by the FDA and other regulatory agencies. It's obvious why the use of an authoritative figure like a doctor or physician was so effective at the time, but it made me wonder—do authoritative individuals in such professions have major influence on what products or services that are adopted by trendsetters, influencers, innovators, and early adopters, these days? And, if so, to what degree?

Going back to the research project mentioned in the previous section, the next part of the questionnaire was focused on a specific category: *Health and Wellness*. The choice of this specific vertical came with a hypothesis: It's tricky for participants to correctly identify what would influence their decision unless it sits within an applicable context. Influence is, after all, very contextual.

You could, for instance, assume that your physician has limited influence on your preference of music, while having greater influence within the context of your health, and so on.

But this is where the insights from the survey surprised us. See Figure 3-4.

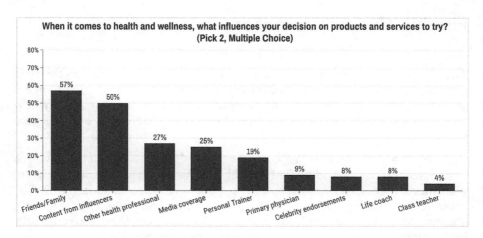

Figure 3-4. Factors that influence product adoption

While it's true that influence is contextual, our friends, family, and—noteworthy—*other social media influencers* outrank both health professionals, personal trainers, and primary physicians combined!

What's going on?

Lots have happened in the world since the 1960s. While Big Tobacco's "doctors recommend" label has been replaced by a Surgeon General's cancer warning, the insights first published in *Diffusion of Innovations* (1962, Rogers) couldn't be more relevant today. Influence might be contextual, with trust functioning as an important variable in its equation, but do you remember the excerpt from the previous section in this chapter, on the importance of peer-to-peer-networks?

The early majority depend on what's conveyed to them from other people that are like them, people that have previously adapted the innovation, and as you've learned, social media influencers are likely to be innovators and early adopters—driving adoption not only among each other but the early majority in particular. You want to influence those with influence? Drive adoption among those that drive early adoption? Get with their friends, their family, and other creators that they follow.

Remember these insights are specific to the group that answered the survey (where the average person is a social media user with, on average, 75,000 followers) and not necessarily reflected by the general population, to help you understand how to *influence those with influence.*

Finding the right creators

"How do I find the right influencers for my brand?"

There's no lack of platforms and tools available that can help you find the right creators, or influencers, for your marketing needs. So why is it still such a challenging task? Back in 2016, my company set out to discover exactly how many talented and creative, influential, individuals that exists on Instagram and YouTube.

Crawling the Web, in a similar fashion to how Google has built their search engine technology, we identified roughly 10 million creators on Instagram with more than 1,000 followers and 2 million YouTube channels with 500 subscribers or more. Now, 10 million people may seem like a lot, but on a platform like Instagram, with more than a billion active users, you're actually looking for a needle in a haystack that sits within the top 1%.

Moreover, most of those 10 million potential creators (or 2 million YouTube channels) will not be relevant for your brand. Consider this breakdown of YouTube channel categories in Table 3-3.

Table 3-3. YouTube channels by category

YouTube, September 2019		
Channel Category[5]	**Channels**	**(%)**
People and blogs	411,296	24%
Gaming	333,997	19%
Entertainment	246,981	14%
Music	206,981	12%
Film and animation	122,273	7%
Comedy	75,269	4%
Education	66,267	4%
How-to and style	66,121	4%
Sports	51,481	3%
Science and technology	35,315	2%
Autos and vehicles	32,647	2%
Travel and events	28,110	2%
News and politics	26,335	2%

(continued)

---

[5] Defined by the owner of that specific YouTube channel

Table 3-3. (*continued*)

YouTube, September 2019		
Channel Category[5]	Channels	(%)
Nonprofits and activism	19,834	1%
Pets and animals	17,700	1%
Shows	1,061	0%
Movies	119	0%
Trailers	116	0%
Total in analyzed dataset	1,741,903	100%

If you're looking to work with YouTube creators within the gaming category, you've suddenly narrowed the potential talent pool by 80%. Want the channel, within that specific category, to be based in a specific market, like the United States? Suddenly, you've narrowed it down to additionally only 25,000 channels or 8% of all gaming channels. Filter by at least 50,000 subscribers, and there are only 3,000 channels left. See Figure 3-5.

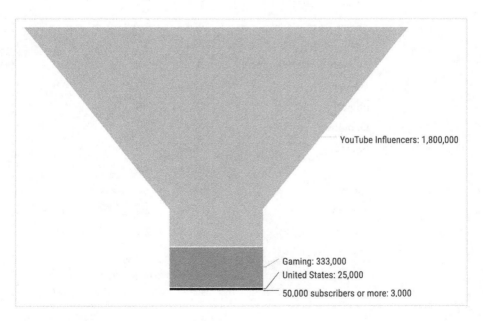

YouTube Influencers: 1,800,000

Gaming: 333,000
United States: 25,000
50,000 subscribers or more: 3,000

Figure 3-5. Top-down funnel, YouTube channels

Okay... 3,000 YouTube gaming channels, in the United States, with at least 50,000 subscribers. That's still a lot in absolute terms, but relative to where we started, you've eliminated 99.9%. This top-down approach is a highly effective way of sizing an opportunity and evaluating the likelihood of identifying talent that fulfill your criteria.

For reference, I've included the same dataset for Instagram, here shown for accounts with more than 1,000 followers with public profiles in Table 3-4.

Table 3-4. Categories on Instagram

Instagram, September 2019		
Category[6]	Count	Share
Fashion	1,151,290	14%
Photography	731,203	9%
Beauty/Makeup	555,295	7%
Travel	527,974	6%
Fitness	504,017	6%
Celebrity	469,046	6%
Luxury Lifestyle	384,767	5%
Business	383,835	5%
Food	375,525	5%
Business and entrepreneurs	370,686	5%
College	322,869	4%
Modeling	305,284	4%
DJ/music	302,139	4%
Brands	295,482	4%
Parent	292,896	4%
Sports	187,704	2%
YouTuber	168,967	2%
Dancer/performer	150,269	2%
Interior design	122,015	1.5%

(continued)

[6] Note that these aren't categories officially endorsed, or used, by Instagram, but rather an analysis and classification based on common types of content. Nevertheless, the table should, in my opinion, be considered highly directionally accurate.

Table 3-4. (*continued*)

Instagram, September 2019		
Category[6]	Count	Share
Tattoo	117,272	1.4%
Wedding	103,394	1.3%
Animals	99,460	1.2%
Pastry	57,127	0.7%
Surf	32,209	0.4%
Motorsports	26,331	0.3%
Skateboard	22,610	0.3%
Real estate	21,291	0.3%
Meme/funny	19,238	0.2%
Gardening	12,338	0.2%
Reality TV	12,190	0.1%
Handicraft	9,329	0.1%
Quotes/inspiration	6,664	0.1%

With this in mind, the rest of this section is spent on setting you up to have the best chance possible of finding the right talent for brand. We'll focus on the variables, characteristics, methodologies, and questions you should address in your quest to find the right talent for your campaign—and you can then seek out the right tools, platforms, or partners that will answer to your needs.

Owning your talent pool

As you've seen, there are millions upon millions of talented and influential content creators across platforms like YouTube and Instagram. And while narrowing your search by using relevant applicable filters—such as category, reach, engagement, demography, audience, and even brand affinity—you can't help but wonder if this is a sustainable long-term strategy. There's nothing wrong with the outcome, but it's an approach where you're starting from scratch every single time, which can be very time consuming and inefficient. So, how do you win this game of finding a needle in a haystack of data?

You play a different kind of game.

Rather than to embark on a quest to find creators and influencers for a specific marketing objective or campaign, your short- and long-term goal should be to build your own pool of talent. Not to be mistaken for an ambassador program (though that could certainly be an outcome), a talent pool is simply a group of individuals that you can activate long and short term, to meet your business and marketing objectives. This approach holds several additional benefits (outlined as follows) and will drive down the overall cost, time, and energy that you spend on your influencer marketing.

The top-down funnel approach is similar to the one mentioned earlier, but the outcome is very different (Figure 3-6).

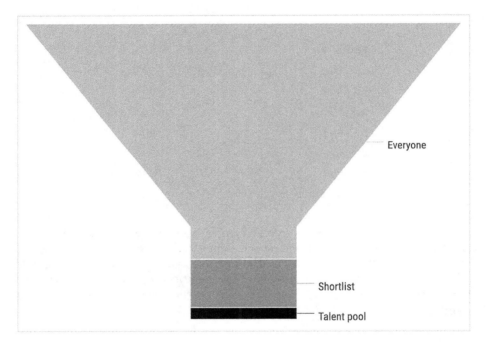

Everyone

Shortlist

Talent pool

Figure 3-6. Top-down funnel, talent pool

The talent pool framework

The ultimate goal of the talent pool strategy is to *increase* your speed of execution, quality, competitive advantage, business impact, and unlock economies of scale. Simultaneously, you'll *reduce* internal politics, risk, and both direct and indirect competition from other brands fighting to work with the same creators. The best part? This is work that can, and should (in my opinion), be carried out well in advance of any specific go-to-market strategies and campaigns and even ahead of any approved media budgets. Your end goal is to build a pool of talented creators, or influencers, ahead of any potential campaign or marketing initiative. This can be coupled with an actual campaign, but it doesn't have to. I'll walk you through the entire process using a fictitious, yet realistic, example.

Direct-to-consumer baby product brand

Markets: United States, United Kingdom

Target audience: Millennial parents

Potential objectives: Content creation, consideration, website sales

Target: Talent pool of 100 creators on Instagram

I'd like to start by studying the endgame. I know my brand, market, audience, objectives, and target. In this example, I'd like to have a talent pool of 100 creators on Instagram that I can activate either short or long term.

Studying the endgame

☐ Talent shortlist is approved by all relevant stakeholders.

☐ Compensation structure in place for every single individual.

☐ Their values, style, and content aligned with my company or marketing goals.

☐ Engagement, reach, and other relevant KPIs align with our potential objectives.

☐ The audience of the talent pool is the right audience.

☐ Responsiveness and affinity—clear expressed interest in working with us.

☐ Proprietary funnel insights (e.g., who drives sales, brand lift, content, etc.).

Don't worry about *how* you'll put all of this in place for now if it seems overwhelming; we'll cover that part later. The first thing we'll do is to identify the overall opportunity. Similar to our prior example of gaming channels on YouTube, it's a top-down approach. It doesn't have to be, but I've found this model to be more effective than the other way around. See Figure 3-7.

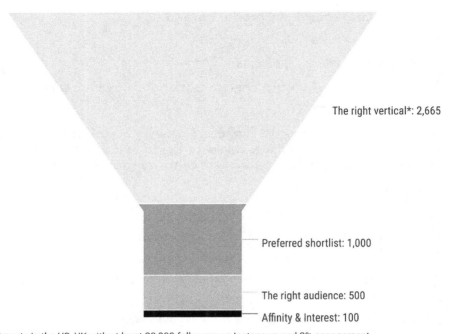

The right vertical*: 2,665

Preferred shortlist: 1,000

The right audience: 500

Affinity & Interest: 100

* Parents in the US, UK with at least 20,000 followers on Instagram and 3% engagement

Figure 3-7. Top-down funnel, Instagram example

As you can see, we've identified a total of **2,665** potential creators within our vertical. They are parents, in our markets, with a sizable following and engaged audience. They don't necessarily align with our values and audience or even have an interest in working with us, but this is just the starting point.

This may seem overwhelming at first (especially if you've never worked with a partner, software as a service, or online platform), but trust me—you'll narrow down the broader selection into a refined shortlist faster than you think. And you're setting yourself up to work with this talent pool long term, so the upfront investment should be considered worthwhile. You're solving the very first bottleneck to unlock an effective and scalable approach to influencer marketing—not just for one campaign, but for years to come.

In microeconomics and business, the concept of *economies of scale* states that a company should be able to achieve a decreased cost per unit when they increase their production or output. This concept can be applied to influencer marketing as well to increase your efficiency. Reduced cost per unit arise from increased total output. Scale drives down cost through strategies like long-term commitment with top performing talent, long-term approach to building a sustainable talent pool (not one-off campaign) drives down your overall cost.

As you narrow your selection, especially if your team is larger than *one*, you'll have to make sure that there's a clear definition of what you're looking for in terms of style, diversity, sentiments, values, and such. There's nothing worse than having one half of your team disapprove what the other half believe is perfect. If you have other stakeholders from other teams weight in with their opinion, make sure that their feedback is assessed objectively.

My next step, in this fictitious example, would be to analyze the audience of my preferred shortlist. To accomplish this, I'd use a third-party company or tool specialized in analyzing and profiling audiences and demographics in social media. A few examples are Demographics Pro,[7] HypeAuditor,[8] and the Audience Insights Tool available from my own company.[9]

Congratulations are in order. We've identified a large pool of talented influencers and creators that we'd like to work with. Your other internal stakeholders have signed off on your shortlist (phew!)—a common bottleneck and time sink, eliminated for the foreseeable future. You and your team can now execute with greater speed than ever before. But remember, our endgame is to have a talent pool of 100 creators with both increased impact and reduced friction. Things are in motion, but the best is yet to come.

A two-way street

In August 2019, my company polled over 2,000 influencers across 67 countries to understand what *their* deciding factors are when seeking out to collaborate with a brand.

Table 3-5. Deciding factors, brand collaboration

Factor	Respondents
How much they pay	14%
That I know their product/service works	27%
That I have heard of their brand before	3%
That their core values are aligned with mine	34%
That they give me creative freedom	23%

Factors such as money, fame, and even creative freedom are outranked by having a shared set of core values. That doesn't mean that those other factors can be ignored, but goes to show that the rigorous vetting process of finding the right creators for your brand will stand or fall by an equally rigorous

---

[7] www.demographicspro.com
[8] www.hypeauditor.com
[9] www.relatable.me/tools-audience-insights-report

vetting process of your brand. Additionally, you'll create a massive unfair advantage for your company if you can demonstrate to influencers and creators that you understand their point of view, something we'll cover in depth in Chapter 5: Creator-Centric Strategies.

This far, we've narrowed down our selection by roughly 80%, from 2,665 to 500 creators. They fit the criteria of our talent pool to perfection. Let's see if the same can be said about our brand. If you examine the top-down funnel numbers outlined in the beginning of our fictitious example, you'll notice that we've planned for a final steep drop-off. As outlined in our previous checklist, you'll want to identify who's responsive and share your core values along with a clearly expressed interest in working with your brand. We took a pass on roughly 80%, so it's only fair to assume that 80% of creators will do the same with us. It's perfectly understood if the process of reaching out to hundreds of influencers just to have *them* qualify *you* may seem overwhelming or even impossible, especially with all the previous work leading up to this stage. We'll cover exactly how to engineer each step of the way in Chapter 6: 1:1 Relationships at Scale. You'll probably be surprised when you realize how easy this part actually is.

Remember, the goal is to have those on your final shortlist raise their hand and let you know if they want to work with your brand as much as you'd like them to work with you. This is also an opportunity to identify other variables that can't be assessed without their input. Do they work out at a local gym? Go to festivals? Like their current smartphone? Own a smartwatch? Use Cannabis? Drink alcohol? Eat meat? Plan to renovate their bathroom? Yes, these are all real examples. And when you know the answer, and they've raised their hand and confirmed that your values are aligned with theirs, you'll never have to look for a needle in a haystack ever again.

From commodity to valuable asset

By narrowing your search from millions, to thousands, to hundreds, you're playing a different kind of game. You now have a talent pool of creators, or influencers, "owned" by your company. Rightfully, these amazing individuals doesn't "belong" to you in any shape or form, but you've transformed a commodity into a valuable asset. But this is just the starting point.

Let's assume that you activate all 100 influencers in your talent pool for a campaign where the goal is to drive sales on your website. Each campaign participant is given a promotional code that their followers can use when they shop on your website. After a week, you analyze the outcome of your campaign. Suddenly, you have a data point and insight that nobody on the planet had last week: You know who sold products and who didn't. You know who the bottom 20% are (that you likely shouldn't engage for a second similar campaign with a similar objective), who the middle 60% are (that help you establish an average benchmark), and who your top performers, the top 20%, are (most valuable distribution, undervalued assets). See Figure 3-8.

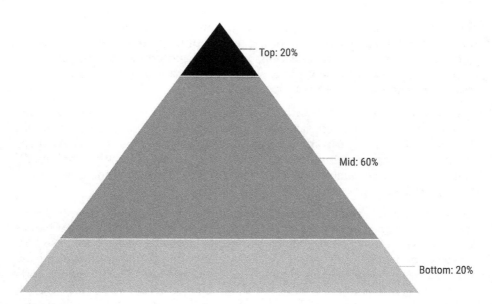

Figure 3-8. From commodity to valuable asset

The same principle can be applied to measure other marketing funnel KPIs like reach, brand lift, website traffic, engagement, website traffic, lead generation, or app installs. If you were to replicate the very same campaign, with the very same structure, and change nothing but to exclude the bottom 20%, you've suddenly skewed the odds to somewhat in your favor. Double down on the top 20%, and you're Billy Beane in *Moneyball*.[10]

The power of the long tail

Amazon, Spotify, and Google have all built their companies on the premise of the long tail. The concept, in the context of business, was popularized in 2004, when *Wired* editor-in-chief Chris Anderson published an article entitled "The Long Tail."[11]

In his article, Anderson argues that our culture and economy is shifting away from a focus on a relatively small number of hits (the head of the demand or distribution curve) toward an infinite, or at least rapidly expanding, number of niches in the tail (collectively with a larger market share than the head). He expanded his reasoning and published a book in 2006, *The Long Tail: Why the Future of Business Is Selling Less of More*. The book entered the *New York Times* bestseller list the same

---

[10] Billy Beane, the baseball general manager whose story was the subject of Michael Lewis' bestselling book *Moneyball: The Art of Winning an Unfair Game*
[11] www.wired.com/2004/10/tail/

year, and the theory of the long tail is since commonly adopted in business, economics, and marketing to explain how a sufficiently large number of niche players (books on Amazon, songs on Spotify, and web pages on Google) can compete with the large powerful few—in a world where markets are decentralized to match unlimited variety of both supply and demand.

I've been fascinated by the long tail since Anderson first published his book, and his theories have personally given me an edge more than once, specifically in web development, e-commerce, and search engine optimization. As such, when co-founding our business in 2016, some 10 years after the book made the bestseller list, I couldn't help but wonder if the very same reasoning could be applied to the world of influencer marketing.

Likely, there'd be a small number of *hits* (social media creators with millions of followers) and a collectively larger number of niches in the tail (social media creators with tens of thousands of followers). Tables 3-6 and 3-7 are based on analysis conducted across the 12,000 most popular social media accounts on Instagram[12] and validate this thesis. There's a clear head (500 creators with more than 10 million followers) and tail (12,000 creators with more than 1 million followers), and that's just the tip of the iceberg. Go further down the tail, and it's evident that the market share of the tail clearly outweighs the head (detailed in Figure 3-9)—and this makes all the difference in the world for us marketing professionals.

Table 3-6. Distribution of creators with more than 1 million followers on Instagram

Followers	Total Creators
10,000,000	500
9,000,000	600
8,000,000	700
7,000,000	800
6,000,000	1,000
5,000,000	1,300
4,000,000	1,800
3,000,000	2,700
2,000,000	5,000
1,000,000	12,000

[12] Internal research project by Relatable, August 2019, N=1,560,000, Global

Table 3-7. Distribution of creators with between 10,000 and 1 million followers on Instagram

Followers	Total Creators
1,000,000	12,000
900,000	13,500
800,000	15,500
700,000	18,000
600,000	22,000
500,000	27,000
400,000	35,000
300,000	50,000
200,000	80,000
100,000	160,000
90,000	190,000
80,000	210,000
70,000	250,000
60,000	300,000
50,000	350,000
40,000	450,000
30,000	550,000
20,000	820,000
10,000	1,500,000

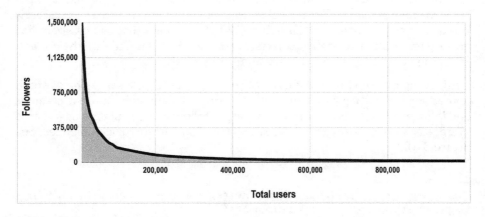

Figure 3-9. The power of the long tail

See, consumers didn't just turn their back on the old model of one-size-fits-all mass appeal—they turned toward something they liked better, something they welcomed with opened arms. For the very first time in their lives, unlimited variety of supply meant that there was that *perfectly tailored something* for *everyone*. When consumers have the option to choose what they paid attention to, they naturally pay more attention.

Between 2015 and 2018, several marketing research companies, influencer marketing agencies, and social media platforms reported that the real power of influencer marketing sits with social media creators on Instagram with a smaller following, loosely referred to as "micro-influencers."

"Micro-Influencers Are More Effective With Marketing Campaigns Than Highly Popular Accounts" reads the headline of an article published by Adweek in 2017.[13]

During the same time, around 2017, I drew the same conclusion. The fewer followers you have on social media, the more engaged the audience. It makes sense when you think about it, as per the theory of the long tail and unlimited variety of supply. This meant two things for marketers. First, there's a greater supply of content creators found in the long tail. Secondly, their audiences are paying closer attention to what they're doing. On the flipside, you'd have to collaborate with a much larger collective of creators to make up for the limited reach and sheer size of each individual audience.

But then, that very same year, something happened: Instagram and its parent company Facebook began, quite literally, to *move things around*. With its most recent update, the order of the posts on a user's feed would no longer show up in chronological order. Instead, their algorithm would switch the order of the posts on a user's feed into what they think each account would like. It sparked some controversy at the time (changing the familiar seems to have that tendency), but came with intentions to improve the way its users experienced their product. The official announcement from Instagram, accurately titled *"See the Moments You Care About First,"* explained that as Instagram had grown, its users had begun to miss out on as much as 70% of their feeds. Including posts they'd actually care about the most.[14]

With complex algorithms in charge of serving its users with engaging content, something interesting happened with the long tail. Suddenly, content creators and influencers with both smaller and larger following began (at an aggregated average, I should note) to see greater attention[15] from their audiences. See Figure 3-10.

---

[13] www.adweek.com/digital/micro-influencers-are-more-effective-with-marketing-campaigns-than-highly-popular-accounts/
[14] https://instagram.tumblr.com/post/141107034797/160315-news
[15] Engagement rate measured by total comments and likes divided by followers

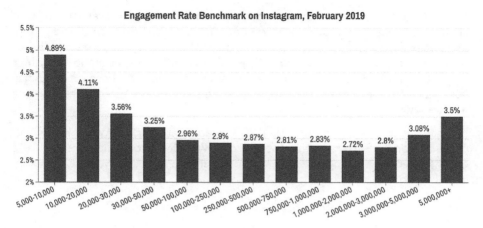

Figure 3-10. Engagement rate benchmark on Instagram, Feb 2019

As indicated by the left side of the graph seen in Figure 4-13, there's a clear correlation between the size of your audience and how engaged they are, but it's only half of the truth. Look to the right side of the graph, and engagement is not just stabilized, but increased. This is the Instagram algorithm at work, serving its users with the posts they actually care about the most. So, has the long tail lost its power? Does the head suddenly have more power than the tail? Judging by the graph, seeking to collaborate with influencers that has an audience of 5 million followers (and an audience just as engaged as someone with 50,000 followers) seems like a no-brainer. Paradoxically, that conclusion would trick you down the wrong path. Perhaps contradictory at first, the tail has even more power than ever before. But remember that these numbers are aggregated averages. There may be more social media creators with a larger following and highly engaged audience, but there aren't that many of them. Consider the following:

Group A

Followers: 5,000,000+

Average engagement: 3.5%

Total creators: 1,300

Group B

Followers: 50,000–100,000

Average engagement: 3%

Total creators: 175,000

On average, if you were to disregard the total number of creators in each group, Group A would be a clear winner. But disregard the size of the group, and you're failing to recognize that the size of the tail is greater than the head. A better question would be how many creators there are, in group B, with at least 3.5% engagement? The answer is more than 48,000. Perhaps an unfair approach to manipulate statistics, but remember we're marketers, not mathematicians.

How about 10% engagement? Still 8,700 creators at your disposal. Meanwhile, there are only 59 users in the entire world with 5 million followers and 10% engagement. The engagement is still found in the long tail; you just have to look closer.

The Art and Science of Creativity

Proven creative strategies for Instagram and YouTube, the seven principles of word of mouth, and the secret to writing a perfect brief

Creative without strategy is called "art." Creative with strategy is called "advertising."

—Jef I. Richards, author and educator

© Aron Levin 2020
A. Levin, *Influencer Marketing for Brands*,
https://doi.org/10.1007/978-1-4842-5503-2_4

Key Questions   How do you pick the right creative strategy for your influencer marketing campaign? What are the key elements of an effective brief? How do you create campaigns that are more likely to generate word of mouth?

Core Principles   1. Great marketing is both science and art. 2. Proven creative executions on Instagram. 4. The creative strategy scorecard. 4. Proven creative executions on YouTube. 5. 17 questions for a highly effective brief. 6. The seven principles of word of mouth.

Creativity—and the act of turning new and imaginative ideas into reality—is a rare form of art. In marketing, it's often the distinction between an idea that outlives its creator and one that never sees the light of day. And while brilliant marketing is a true form of art, it's also a science.

It's challenging to outline a bulletproof framework for creative work, as the definition of the word itself is "to imagine original ideas." With that in mind, my job in this chapter will be to outline both the science (strategy) and the art (inspiration). Your job is to mash them up and create *magic*.

You'll learn 14 proven campaign strategies for Instagram followed by 9 different ways to create content on YouTube. I'll even give you a scientific model for how to pick the right campaign strategy every single time. We'll return to these creative strategies in Chapter 7: The Four-Step Influencer Marketing Framework where you'll see how everything comes together. You'll learn the seven principles of word of mouth—and how to incorporate each principle with your creative strategy. Then, I'll break down the components of the brief template that we have used within my company across more than 10,000 collaborations between influencers and brands. Ready?

THE SEVEN QUESTIONS THAT LEAD TO CREATIVITY

The following questions (see Chapter 7: The Four-Step Influencer Marketing Framework for details) can help spark your creativity and identify a message that resonates with creators, their community, and your customers.

1.   Do you have any unique insights about your target audience or your industry?

2.   What is the opportunity, based on those insights?

3.   What's popular and relevant in culture, right now?

4.   What would connect with your audience at a deeper level and cross-cultural borders?

5.   What would create an emotional connection with the public?

6.   What would have value as a topic of discussion, due to being resonant and meaningful?

7.   What would engage, polarize, provoke, or entertain the audience of the creator?

14 proven creative executions on Instagram

The days where you could get someone on Instagram to post a selfie with a product placement and a discount code in the caption aren't necessarily over—but it's sure not as effective as it was in 2012. That year, Instagram had 10 million users. Fast-forward to mid-2018, and the number had grown to 1 billion monthly active users[1]. The platform evolved, as did the way brands use the platform to collaborate with its most talented and influential creators.

I've witnessed firsthand how challenging and overwhelming this transition has been for our clients. Even our own team of business developers and campaign operators suffered from the rapid pace of feature deployment when, in less than a year, Instagram launched Stories, Shopping, Polls, and Live Video.

Meanwhile, the campaigns became more complex, and what started off as relatively straightforward execution quickly became very challenging to manage. Initially, clients came with relatively simple requests, like if they could pick which hashtag creators would use to promote their product launch. But then, from nowhere, they'd ask for branded experiences through Instagram Live or driving product preference through story polls. It became impossible to keep up, and something had to change, fast.

On the other hand, after having worked on hundreds of campaigns, with thousands of creators and influencers, a pattern began to emerge. Most campaigns, it turns out, would deploy one or several of the same strategies. After careful examination and analysis, we identified a total of 14 different campaign strategies for influencer marketing on Instagram. Nine times out of ten, these strategies would cover pretty much any campaign objective, creative angle, or strategy, each with its own set of example uses, key benefits, and sometimes drawbacks.

By the time you're reading this, it's likely that a thing or two has changed or evolved, but they've held true for over two years at this point, the online equivalent of a decade in the offline world.

---

[1] https://techcrunch.com/2018/06/20/instagram-1-billion-users/

Your brand, product, audience, messaging, goals, and campaign objectives are all variables that will dictate which of these strategies will be effective. It's also common that several of them (between two and five) are applied for the same campaign.

The 14 different creative executions, or strategies, for influencer marketing on Instagram are as follows:

1. Single Feed Post Campaign
2. Story-Only Campaign
3. Pairing Feed Posts and Stories
4. Multi-post Campaign (Ambassador Program)
5. Amplifying Brand Experiences
6. Burst Campaigns
7. Going Live for Maximum Authenticity
8. Supporting Hero Brand Campaigns
9. Driving Consideration Through Polls
10. Hyper Local Campaigns
11. Swipe-Up Lead Generation
12. Real-Time Recruitment
13. Creating Content for Ads
14. Using Influencers as Talent

We'll go through what each strategy entails along with example uses and key benefits. To help further, you'll be assisted by a scorecard for additional support at the end of this section—but you'll have to become familiar with the traits of each and trust your gut feeling as well.

Creative strategy 1: Single Feed Post Campaign

Single Feed Post Campaigns allow for brands to work with the maximum number of people within their budget.

Example uses:

*   Driving mass awareness around a new product
*   High-quality beauty shots incorporating the brand/product

- Using influencers to quickly create high-quality content to fill brand social media calendar

Key benefits:

- The most cost-efficient way to test-out influencer marketing.

- Working with a range of people for the campaign offers a number of different ways to portray the brand.

- If aiming for content creation, creates a wide range of high-quality in-feed content to choose from.

Creative strategy 2: Story-Only Campaign

Story-Only Campaigns deliver the brand message in a raw way without the polish of the feed posts, which for some brands is exactly what they are looking for. Also they allow for the most influencers for the budget.

Example uses:

- Demonstrating how influencers use the product

- Driving click-through to a landing page

- Creating a sneak-peak look of a new product

- Promoting a live experience

Key benefits:

- Working with a range of people for the campaign offers a number of different ways to portray the brand.

- Raw storytelling format can feel more authentic.

- Click-through rates are significantly better than in-feed.

Notable caveats:

- Too many stories in a clip can cause audiences to swipe away.

Creative strategy 3: Pairing Feed Posts and Stories

Mixing behind-the-scene story content with high-quality feed post content tells a fuller brand story.

Example uses:

- Showing a final product or look in a feed post paired with a how-to set of clips through stories

- Brand-storytelling through many stories, paired with an influencer-created hero image in the feed post that can be reused for content

Key benefits:

- Allows for multiple types of storytelling both raw and polished

- Reach consumers with the same messaging in two different formats

Creative strategy 4: Multi-post Campaign (Ambassadorship)

Ambassadorships allow the influencers to tell a deeper brand story and show how they incorporate the brand into multiple touchpoints in their lives through multiple formats over a duration of weeks or months.

Example uses:

- Storytelling around the many features of a product or location over time

- Showing continued usage, demonstrating progress, or onboarding brand affinity as a result of using a product

Key benefits:

- Enables long-term storytelling about the different ways the brand can be experienced.

- Allows multiple brand exposures to each creator's audience, ensuring both reach and frequency.

- Influencers will give a discount when creating multiple posts.

- Reinforces impact as the ongoing support strengthens influencer-brand connection.

Creative strategy 5: Amplifying Brand Experiences

Brand experiences are now engineered specifically to be Instagram worthy for all the attendees; however, sometimes the beautiful installations don't tell the full brand story themselves. Properly briefed influencers can tell this missing story.

Example uses:

- Influencers can create excitement before, during, and after an event, all while delivering various brand messages through a mixture of Instagram stories that tell the raw story and feed posts that capture the hero shot of the event.

- Influencers can be used to be the "street photographers" of a brand experience, creating content for a carousel that tells the many parts of the event while also generating high-quality content for brand social feeds.

Key benefits:

- Allows brands to extend the reach of their events to larger audiences

- Briefed influencers tell exactly the story you want to tell rather than just "hoping" people understand the point of the event or even know what it is celebrating.

- Influencers create content that looks like content people like and share (it's why they are influencers). This is naturally a perfect fit for brand social channels.

Creative strategy 6: Burst Campaigns

An influencer gets reach, a crew gets noticed. Burst Campaigns are all about making an impact with a crew of influencers than can effectively blanket the Instagram feeds of their targeted users.

Example uses:

- Burst Campaigns are perfect for product launches, as 30–300 influencers all posting the same day will surely cut through the digital clutter.

- Burst Campaigns can also strongly support a large brand campaign by mirroring the message of the campaign with an act of influencers that support the campaign message.

Key benefits:

- In this instance, the whole is greater than the sum of its parts, as the frequency of this type of campaign creates a sense in the consumers that they are missing out on something that all these influencers are talking about—driving increased consideration.
- By focusing the content on a single day, the impact is clear, rather than diluted over the course of weeks or months.

Creative strategy 7: Going Live for Maximum Authenticity!

Instagram Live is simply an uncut version of the truth, which makes it both interesting and a bit scary!

Example uses:

- An ongoing live moment with an influencer (e.g., morning routine)
- Highlighting a hero moment of a brand event
- Capturing real-time interactions of consumers

Key benefits:

- Unrivaled authenticity

Notable caveats:

- Cannot plan for unscripted moments
- Need to promote the "live event" so audiences know to tune in

Creative strategy 8: Supporting Hero Brand Campaigns

Hero brand campaigns are typically rooted in a big idea that reflects the persona and ideals of the brand, not just information about the product. Influencers can be used to bring this idea to life in a relatable context, becoming an incredibly powerful leg of a brand campaign execution.

Example uses:

- Recruiting influencers to interpret their own connection to the statement made in the brand campaign

- Using influencers to react to the brand campaign and talk about what it means to them

- Integrating influencers as the core idea of the campaign, enlisting them to both create the content but also distribute it

Key benefits:

- Reinforcing the same brand message across multiple touchpoints is one of the core tenets of strong marketing.

- Aligns influencer marketing as a core part of a campaign media strategy rather than just something added on after.

Creative strategy 9: Driving Consideration Through Polls

It's amazing what the world will give you if you just ask. Instagram Story Polls are one of the most effective marketing tools on any channel through directly engaging audiences.

Example uses:

- Drive increased brand consideration by asking consumers to choose between two products—inherently establishing a preference in their minds as they make a selection.

- Create story polls to ask consumers about their opinions of a brand during the first post of a multi-post engagement, and then poll them again in the last to see how the brand consideration changed.

Key benefits:

- Not only do Instagram Story Polls drive very strong engagement; they also produce valuable information to the brand.

- Benchmarks show nearly 10% engagement, 4x the average on Instagram for feed posts.

Creative strategy 10: Hyper Local Campaigns

Some products are closely tied to specific locations, such as restaurants, tourist attractions, or limited availability products. By having talented creators visit these locations, the story you tell and content you produce will naturally be both authentic and engaging.

Example uses:

- Restaurant that wants to promote a specific item on a menu at a location

- Hotel or resort that wants to promote specific features of that location

- Brand or product that wants to highlight the availability of a product in a certain place

Key benefits:

- This is a type of marketing that is unique to influencers— it's real on-the-ground word of mouth, amplified by social media.

- Influencers will be talking about their own, genuine experiences at these locations, so the content is extremely authentic.

Creative strategy 11: Swipe-Up Lead Generation

The main KPIs for Instagram campaigns are typically reach and engagement, rather than direct sales. However, it's possible to set up campaigns to feed another portion of the marketing funnel and measure success through the cost per lead and the cost difference of influencer-referred leads and those targeted by other means.

Example uses:

- Influencer content can drive to a brand page allowing the brand to retarget that consumer through existing Facebook or display campaign funnels.

- Alternately, we can drive to an email-sign up page, allowing the brand to enter the leads into an email marketing campaign.

Key benefits:

- For high-priced items or FMCG brands looking for more than just reach and engagement from influencers, this setup allows them to do performance marketing through Instagram that's not just connected to direct sales.

- No one buys something the first time they see it, so this approach allows us to power the rest of the marketing funnel by starting with the strongest trigger in marketing: word of mouth.

Creative strategy 12: Real-Time Recruitment

Brands love to talk about their involvement with big cultural moments and are willing to invest in bringing ambassadors to these events to promote the brand's involvement. Real-Time Recruitment is a way to maximize the amount spent on influencers, as opposed to flights and hotels.

Example uses:

- Recruiting influencers that are at a high-impact festival or summer destination to post content on behalf of the brand.

Key benefits:

- Why spend money on getting influencers to an event if there are some already there? The key is to use technology to find them.

Creative strategy 13: Creating Content for Ads

Influencers have generated their large followings by creating highly relevant, inspiring, and engaging content—exactly the type of creative work brands turn to their creative agencies for. Influencers can be used to create their own translation of the brand's message, and the brand can then negotiate the rights for commercial reuse.

Example uses:

- Create highly engaging social content for a new product, reusing and promote, only content that received high-organic reach, ensuring marketing spend is allocated efficiently.

Key benefits:

- Influencer marketing is already an incredibly cost-effective way at generating brand content. After the content is already produced and is well-received by audiences, it makes sense to want to use that content for larger audiences.

Creative strategy 14: Using Influencers as Talent

Influencers in fashion and lifestyle verticals already have zeitgeist-defining looks. When producing brand created content, using influencers as talent not only gets you camera-ready talent, but also the reach of the influencers as they talk about the shoot. This is not something we've done yet; however, it is a compelling idea.

Example uses:

- Casting foreground or background talent in the TV commercials or social media shoots
- Using a camera crew to film influencers as they are used in other activations, such as brand experiences

Key benefits:

- Influencers can be contracted to post about the shoot (although many will do so organically).
- Fans of the influencers will want to see the brand content to see their favorite influencers in it.

The creative strategy scorecard

As you can see, each of these creative executions and campaign types has its own set of benefits, example uses, and sometimes even shortcomings. To make sense of it all, you can rank their different benefits by order of relevance based on their different characteristics, mapped to the circumstances or conditions of a specific brand, or your unique campaign goals. Figure 4-1 shows a scorecard.

	1. Single Feed Post Campaign	2. Story Only Campaign	3. Pairing Feed posts and Stories	4. Multi Post Campaign (Ambassadorship)	5. Amplifying brand experiences	6. Burst Campaigns	7. Going Live for maximum authenticity	8. Supporting Hero Brand Campaign	9. Driving consideration through Polls	10. Hyper Local Campaigns	11. Swipe-up Lead Generation	12. Real-time Recruitment	13. Creating Content for Ads	14. Using Influencers as Talent
A. Are you launching a new product?	✓	✓	✓			✓			✓					
B. Are you looking to integrate influencer marketing as a part of a bigger brand campaign?	✓	✓	✓		✓	✓		✓						
C. Are you planning a branded experience or event?		✓	✓		✓		✓			✓				
D. Do you advertise on Facebook?													✓	
E. Do you ever sponsor or integrate your marketing with culturally relevant happenings, such as festivals or location-specific happenings?		✓	✓		✓							✓		
F. Does your product/service depend on site-specific availability (e.g. retail, gym, event)?		✓					✓			✓				✓
G. Do you have a very specific criteria for influencer selection that historically have made it very complicated to identify potential talent, or do you think that this will be the case?			✓	✓						✓				
H. Do you sell your product direct-to-consumers, online?			✓			✓					✓		✓	
I. Is a large portion of your existing marketing driven by organic word of mouth?			✓	✓		✓								
J. Are you new to influencer marketing?	✓	✓												
K. Is your product an app available on App Store or Google Play?	✓	✓									✓		✓	
L. Is your product complex or require in-depth storytelling to be appreciated or understand?	✓	✓	✓				✓		✓					

Figure 4-1. Creative strategy scorecard

As you can see, the different questions (A–L) are now mapped to the creative execution if it is applicable.

Let's say you're launching a new product (Question A). If the answer is yes, both Burst Campaigns (#6 on the list), Poll (#9), and Single Feed Post (#1) would, more often than not, be relevant creative strategies. Is your product complex, and does it require in-depth storytelling to be fully understood (Question M)? Then, Story-Only Campaigns (#2), Pairing Feed Posts and Stories (#3), Going Live for Maximum Authenticity (#7), and Driving Consideration Through Polls (#9) would all be applicable.

I highly encourage the use of the scorecard to evaluate the level of relevancy of each applicable strategy. You also have access to a free online tool[2] that will help you evaluate each strategy, along with a high-resolution version of the printed chart.[3]

Nine proven creative executions on YouTube

YouTube and Google have published their own official guidelines and suggestions[4] with an outline of nine different and proven creative executions for brands that seek to work with the millions of talented creators on their video platform.

On YouTube, it's common practice for brands, creators, and their agents or agencies to distinguish between *dedicated* and *integrated* videos. *Dedicated* videos are branded collaborations between creators and brands where your product or service is the only one featured in a video. Examples include tutorials, unboxing, lookbooks, branded storytelling, product demos, or sketches. *Integrated* videos mention your brand, but would also feature other content, products, or brands. Examples of use would include hauls,[5] favorite products, unboxing, or contextually relevant shout-outs/mentions of your brand.

Let's review the nine common types of content creation on YouTube and how they can be used to build collaborations between brands and creators.

---

[2] https://rlt.to/strategy
[3] Go to www.apress.com/9781484255025
[4] www.thinkwithgoogle.com/features/youtube-playbook/topic/partnering-with-creators/
[5] A video recording, in which a person discusses items that they recently purchased, sometimes going into detail about their experiences during the purchase and the cost of the items they bought

Product Tutorial/Demo Video

A tutorial or product demo is a video showcasing how your product works by highlighting features and functions. Similar to a story campaign on Instagram, it works great for more complex products. The collaboration can be either integrated or dedicated, but keep in mind that the video should be focused on providing value for the audience, and integrate any promotional aspects in a subtle and authentic way. Further, if done correctly, tutorial videos can have an almost eternal shelf life—harnessing the power of the recommendation algorithm on YouTube—and help brands accumulate views over a longer period of time.

Product Review, Hauls, and Unboxing Videos

Next up are three popular creative executions, all covered within the same section of this chapter because of their similar traits. Chances are that you've run across all three in the past.

In a product review video, the creator gives their honest opinion and rating of your product. Video product reviews can be powerful conversion drivers, and a recent study has shown that more than half (55%) of consumers that search for a product on Google learn more by going to YouTube before they make a purchase.[6] Another study from 2015 found that 57% of shoppers watch product review videos the week before they buy consumer electronic products.[7]

While unboxing videos may have been popularized by the technology and electronics category, it can certainly be an effective format within other categories as well, like the makeup, wellness, and beauty industry. Video marketing firm Sponsokit found that 86% of the top 200 beauty videos on YouTube were all made by creators, as opposed to brands,[8] and research data from Google have shown that that product research is on the rise both across low-consideration and high-consideration product categories[9]—ranging from deodorants to travel accessories and even umbrellas.

For a product review or unboxing video to be successful, it's important to allow for creators to voice their honest opinion—or you may risk alienating the audience or, even worse, have the entire collaboration backfire, like in the

---

[6] Source: Google/Magid Advisors, Global (US, CA, BR, UK, DE, FR, JP, IN, KR, AU), "The Role of Digital Video in People's Lives," n=20,000, A18–64 general online population, August 2018

[7] Google Millward Brown CE Study, n=1,529 CE shoppers, January 2015. Correction, October 29, 2015

[8] https://medium.com/sponsokit/more-people-than-ever-are-turning-to-youtube-for-product-reviews-4956d3647e34

[9] www.thinkwithgoogle.com/consumer-insights/consumer-mobile-search-buying-behavior/

case of when YouTuber iTwe4kz sent headphone manufacturer KANOA into bankruptcy.[10] The company allegedly tried to bribe Cody (also known as iTwe4kz) for positive coverage, to which he responded with a brutal 27-minute video[11] to his 600,000 subscribers.

In a collaboration with the popular technology review YouTuber, KANOA sent a pair of headphones to the tech YouTuber to review, but the headphones he received didn't work, to which he reached out with a request for a new pair. Fair enough, you'd think. Instead, they offered to pay him 500 dollars for a positive review. Rather than taking them up on the offer, the suggestion triggered a different response:

> You want me to put my integrity on the line so that you can sell some of these pieces of shit [headphones]? Are you kidding me? Five hundred dollars? No you can't give me five hundred and I'll put out a good review. This is trash!

Note that the problem isn't the collaboration, compensation, or even the faulty product, but the lack of transparency and authenticity. Consumers expect brands to collaborate with creators and creators to showcase their products—but remember why they turned to their channel in the first place:

Because they trust their opinion. Ask for an honest review of a product that doesn't work, and you can expect what you asked for.

Lookbook

A lookbook is a stylized video where a creator showcases multiple products from one brand—typically within fashion, clothing, and makeup. Integrate your collaboration in upcoming culturally relevant calendar events and themes, such as Back to School, Spring, or Fall. Alternatively, you can theme your lookbook videos to specific audiences or contexts, such as Work, Plus Size, or Date Night. All these examples are from most popular search suggestions on YouTube—a tactic that can help generate video ideas that are more likely to resonate with a specific audience. There's another upside to this approach as well, namely, that YouTube creators place great value in video ideas that will resonate with their audience and are more inclined to work with those that have a good understanding of what will attract new and existing subscribers.

---

[10] https://fortune.com/2017/08/27/headphone-startup-kanoa-youtube-review/
[11] https://youtu.be/36Gw3tErUSM

Memes and Comedy Sketch

The word *meme* was first coined by British scientist Richard Dawkins in his 1976 book *The Selfish Gene*, defined as "a unit of cultural transmission."[12]

He writes: "Memes (discrete units of knowledge, gossip, jokes and so on) are to culture what genes are to life. Just as biological evolution is driven by the survival of the fittest genes in the gene pool, cultural evolution may be driven by the most successful memes."

Nowadays, memes are synonymous with funny images, videos, or gifs that are copied and spread like viruses in social media and online, often with slight variations—but the origin of the word actually derives from the Greek *mimēma*, "that which is imitated."

Sure, when you think of memes, Grumpy Cat, Rickrolling, and Success Kid all come to mind. But the idea of a meme—an imitation of an idea that is relevant in culture—can also function as the core foundation of a creative strategy. This isn't the same as making a video that will "go viral" (which, for the record, is a silly strategy), but rather to build on something that is popular in culture or that can be replicated in different variations, with various degrees of success.

In 2016, for instance, several YouTubers in the fitness industry joined "The 10,000 Calorie Challenge." As the name suggests, the challenge involved documenting the process of consuming 5x the amount of the recommended daily amount of calories. Search the phrase on YouTube, and you'll find thousands of videos, with millions of views, with an entire community of creators imitating each other and a clear opportunity for brands to create both integrated and dedicated videos and participate in the transmission of culture.

Creative concepts can be developed to allow for imitation as well. In 2018, direct-to-consumer brand BURST Oral Care first teamed up with Khloe Kardashian to publish a series of stories and videos on Instagram demonstrating the effectiveness of their electric toothbrush. But rather than brushing her teeth, the demonstration of the product is carried out on a cob of corn covered in coffee grounds.

When you see a video thumbnail of Khloe Kardashian, Chrissy Teigen, or one of the many celebrities and YouTubers that have since participated in *The Burst Corn Challenge*, and they pose with a toothbrush and corn on the cob covered in coffee, you can't help but wonder what's going on. A creative concept that can be replicated and imitated again and again, a challenge started as a brand collaboration, but has since been replicated organically by both customers and other YouTubers.

---

[12] Richard Dawkins, *The Selfish Gene* (Oxford University Press, 1976)

Game Play

This one is popular, for obvious reasons, within the gaming community. In this type of video, the gamer plays through several levels or an entire game, typically with commentary on what they are experiencing and their review

Brand/Product Shout-Out

A mention of your brand, product, or service, for example, "I partnered with [Brand Name] to bring you this video," typically in the very beginning of a video and at the end.

Favorites

Creator dedicates an entire video around a theme that they are excited about and is currently relevant, for example, "My favorite back to school items." Similar to lookbook videos, you can leverage the search suggestions on YouTube to generate ideas for video topics.

Writing an effective brief

One of the cornerstones to succeed with your influencer marketing campaigns or programs is to write an effective brief to influencers and creators. What follows is a list of questions that you'll want to answer to help your counterpart understand what is required from them. See section "Constrained by communication" in Chapter 6: 1:1 Relationships at Scale for more information.

1. Who are you and your company? (introduction)

2. What does your company, product, or service do? (background)

3. Why are you reaching out to me? (context)

4. What is expected of me? (brief)

5. When is it expected? (commitment)

6. How will we be working together? (process)

7. How much will I get paid? (compensation)

8. What do you want me to do next? (call to action)

9. How will this help me create content for my audience? (benefits)

10. Any chance that this could hurt my career or personal brand? (risks)

11. Are there other benefits for me that I should know? (benefits)

12. How do I know that I can trust you? (risk)

13. Who else have you worked with? (social proof and community)

14. How much time will this take? (commitment)

15. When will I get paid? (terms)

16. What are your marketing goals? (objective)

17. What makes your product/service special? (unique selling points)

Brief template

Over the last three years, my company has developed a proven brief template that has been successfully used in thousands of collaborations on Instagram, across pretty much any category and vertical that you could possibly imagine. What follows is the exact email template we use, how each element of the brief is structured, and how to address each of the 17 questions.

Subject: Invite to paid Instagram campaign with [brand name]

Hi @creator,

[your name] from [your company] here.

[Short two-sentence intro to spark enough interest to keep reading. You can mention other creators or influencers you've worked with here, but keep it very brief.]

If you're interested, read on for all the info. At the bottom you'll find a button you tap to register your participation. If you have any questions, don't hesitate to reach out.

/Aron

—INVITATION TO COLLABORATE WITH [BRAND]—

About [brand]

Two short sentences about your brand. If you're promoting a specific product, describe its key benefits and unique selling points.

About the campaign

Explain the campaign in two paragraphs. What is the background to the campaign? Is this a part of a bigger marketing initiative? What is asked from the creator, in summary? (You'll provide detailed instructions in the next sections of the brief.) This section should, effectively, sell the idea of the campaign help the creator understand if what you're suggesting is relevant and interesting enough to continue reading.

The goal of the campaign

Explain the goals of the campaign and what you're hoping to achieve by working together. How will you define success of the campaign?

Your instructions

This information is personally tailored for the owner of the Instagram account @creator.

You need to do this

- What will the creator need to do to deliver on the campaign creative brief? Use your product? Install an app? Visit a specific location? Etc.

- Create content for [#] story and [#] post according to the guidelines below

- Send your content for approval before [date].

- Publish your approved content on [date].

- Include the following in your post: #collaboration #campaign @mention.

- Any feed posts need to remain on your account for 30 days. Any stories need to remain on your account for their full 24 hours.

- You may not publish any sponsored posts or stories for another brand 24 hours before or after the publication date in this campaign.

- Your caption should be in the language you usually post in.

- It's important that you follow the guidelines below. 👇 👇 👇

In exchange you will get this

- You will be paid [amount] for participating in this campaign. You will need to take care of social fees and other taxes on your own. Contact your local tax authority to find out how.

- The amount will be paid when we've confirmed that you've followed all the guidelines. You will then also receive all the information you need on how to get your payment.
- Please allow up to 14 days to receive your payment.

Guidelines for your [total number of] posts

In-Feed Post

- Include detailed instructions in bullet points to provide creative guidelines.
- Mention what should be included in the picture and what should be avoided.

Caption

- Start your caption with #ad or the equivalent.
- Mention that [talking points].
- Highlight [important considerations].
- Call to action: Encourage your followers to [call to action].

Story (4+ clips in video format or whatever you're asking for)

- What is the creative direction? Example: Show some "behind the scenes" on how you [creative direction...].
- Call to action: Encourage your followers to [call to action].
- Please make sure to include the hashtags and swipe up link in all clips.

Inspiration

Include an example caption or links to previous successful collaborations.

Finally, include a 3 × 3 moodboard with nine inspirational photos.

To join the campaign, [click here/write me back/or other call to actions].

This email template, in some varying degree of course (to address the unique circumstances of each campaign), has been used successfully in over 10,000 collaborations on Instagram and YouTube. Can it be improved further? For sure, but it gets the job done every single time.

I know what you might be thinking though…because the most common response from brands and marketing professionals when they see this is that the brief is too detailed, too long. Nobody will read it, and so on. First, that's wrong. I've witnessed firsthand how this template has been used across thousands of collaborations. Secondly, creators frequently express how thankful they are for getting their questions answered upfront, with full clarity. Why? It answers each of the 17 questions, in a structured, easy-to-read, format.

Remember, you can include additional information about your product and detailed do's and don'ts for you campaign, once someone has confirmed that they want to work with you; just make sure that the scope of the campaign remain the same.

The YouTube creator's creative brief

YouTube has, in their official brand and creator guidelines, published a six-step guide to writing an effective creator's creative brief, available on their website.[13] They recommend that brands include the following essential elements: Objective, Insight, Style and Messaging, Deliverables, Inclusions, and Creative Control.

Objective

What is the purpose of the campaign and what are you hoping to achieve? Key considerations in this first element include your challenges, goals, and insights used to inform the strategy. YouTube suggests that you're as clear and specific as possible and focus on the role the creator will play in the overall campaign. Further, it helps to provide competitive benchmarks and define which metrics you will use to determine if the campaign is successful.

Insight

What key insight can you provide so that the creator can develop a compelling storyline for their video? If possible, include insights, data, market, or consumer insights, who your brand is specifically trying to reach.

Style and messaging

What is the personality of your brand? Are there talking points, key messaging, phrasing, or words that you'd want the creator to include in their video? This element of the brief will help ensure brand consistency.

---

[13] www.thinkwithgoogle.com/features/youtube-playbook/topic/partnering-with-creators/

Deliverables

What is the final deliverable required by the creator? Where will the video be published, and what rights are you asking for?

Inclusions

Are there certain must-haves in your video or things to avoid? Further, YouTube suggests that brands outline brand safety requirements, monetization settings, FTC Compliance, and category exclusivity. It's important to address any requirements before signing contracts or initiating content production.

Creative control

Finally, what creative control does the creator have? Provide detailed feedback up front and during content review to avoid reshoots or long feedback cycles.

Word of mouth

What do Space X, Bitcoin, Spotify, Uber, Slack, Flappy Bird (You do remember Flappy Bird, right?), and Amazon Prime all have in common?

Incredible growth—driven primarily by word of mouth.

Their users, customers, loyal fans, and their brand ambassadors can't seem to keep their mouths shut—and that's a good thing! But what is it, specifically, that makes a product or service like those earlier examples, talk-worthy? Are there commonly shared attributes among these examples that make them more likely to be successful?

And if that would be the case, can we, as marketers, break down the elements and incorporate their principles into our creative development (and even product development) to be more likely to succeed?

Do you remember when your friends told you about the app where you could press a button and have a private driver arrive within minutes?[14] The music-streaming service that would have you play any song on demand,[15] for free, instantaneously? The annoyingly simple yet addictive little mobile game with the flapping bird[16]? The bird that drove everyone—including its creator—crazy.

---

[14] www.uber.com
[15] www.spotify.com
[16] https://mashable.com/2014/02/10/flappy-bird-story/

Flappy Bird conquered the world; its Vietnamese founder Dong Nguyen lost his mind and took the app off the App Store. But do you remember when it first exploded all over Twitter and then blew up in the news? These things, seemingly random, are not.

Having spent more than five years at music-streaming service Spotify, working specifically with user growth (and prior to Spotify at King Digital Entertainment, the maker of Candy Crush—another great example that could fit into the previously mentioned list of successful products), I've had the unfair advantage of getting to study these things firsthand, as they were taking place, with access to all the relevant data and insights that an outsider wouldn't have.

Seven principles of word of mouth

When I began to break down what caused certain products and services to be more talked about than others, I found that the more of the following principles you could apply, the more likely your brand, product, or service (or marketing campaign) would be to gain traction through word of mouth.

See, the best marketing in the world (specifically influencer marketing) doesn't have to be overly creative to drive exceptional buzz or word of mouth. Instead, it can be dressed down to a point where you're amplifying a message that is already out there in the market that resonates with the audience you're aiming to reach.

It sure isn't a one-size-fits-all solution, nor is it always easy, but can be extremely powerful when appropriately applied.

Speaking of applied insights, you may wonder what this has to do with influencer marketing, and the context and contents of this book? In short, if the core message in your campaign can tick these boxes, then the engagement in your campaign, the earned media aspect, and the amplified word of mouth will improve dramatically.

As such, you can identify if you've developed a creative idea, value proposition, or communication strategy that people will talk about, by asking yourself the following seven questions. You don't need to answer each and every one with a yes, but the better they're aligned, the greater your chances. The questions are:

1. Does it solve a problem?
2. Is it easy to talk about?
3. Does it feel good to share?
4. Does it evoke a sense that the world is an amazing place?
5. Does it start a conversation?

6.   Is it relevant to our core target audience?

7.   Once experienced, does it exceed your expectations?

It, in this scenario, is your product, service, value proposition, idea, or creative campaign. Go back to the list in the beginning of this section (Space X, Spotify, Uber, Bitcoin, Slack, Flappy Bird, and Amazon Prime), and ask yourself these seven questions, and you'll see how the answer, more often than not, is a yes.

How about commercial messages and advertising? Search for "Top Ad Campaign of the 21st Century"[17] and you'll see that the list by AdAge is featuring campaigns like:

•   Dumb Ways to Die

•   Apple: Get a Mac

•   Red Bull: Stratos

•   Dove: Campaign for Real Beauty.

•   Old Spice: The Man Your Man Could Smell Like

Check them out, go back to the questions, and you'll see that these principles can be applied to some of the most iconic adverts ever produced (they seem to be the ones most frequently shared, as well). So what *problem (question #1)* does the now iconic Old Spice commercial [featuring Isaiah Mustafa on a white horse][18] solve?

It spoke to women, without alienating men.

Meanwhile, the Red Bull Stratos[19] campaign did, indeed, evoke a sense that the world is an amazing place or, to use their own words, "to advance scientific discoveries in aerospace for the benefit of mankind."[20]

Does it feel good to share the Dumb Ways to Die video[21]? In fact, it's so entertaining that they turned into not one but two mobile games. Did the iconic Get a Mac[22] campaign start a conversation relevant to its core target segment? For sure, and it helped Apple sell more computers and increase their market share.[23]

These creative ideas solve problems, are easy to talk about, feel good to share, evoke a sense that the world is an amazing place, start conversations,

---

[17] http://adage.com/lp/top15/

[18] www.youtube.com/watch?v=owGykVbfgUE

[19] www.youtube.com/watch?v=raiFrxbHxVO

[20] www.redbullstratos.com/the-mission/what-is-the-mission/

[21] www.youtube.com/watch?v=IJNR2EpSOjw

[22] www.adweek.com/creativity/apples-get-mac-complete-campaign-130552/

[23] www.workingpsychology.com/download_folder/GAM_Campaign_Analysis.pdf

are relevant to a core target segment of customers, and exceed our expectations as consumers.

It's to be noted that there's naturally a varying degree of problem-solving, conversation-starting, and feel-good involved in each of these examples—what's important is to have your messaging and creative ideas align with as many of these principles as possible to create better impact.

Let's break down the seven core principles of word of mouth and uncover how each can be applied to your own creative development.

Principle 1. Solving a problem

Products and services that solve problems better than anything else will naturally have an organic intake of new users. Uber is an amazing example; Slack is another. Space X is solving the problem of saving humanity while Spotify is making the world's music accessible to everyone.

But this can also be in the form of entertainment (Flappy Bird, Candy Crush) or your way of communicating an issue or culturally relevant topic (Old Spice: The Man Your Man Could Smell Like, Dove: Campaign for Real Beauty[24]).

For influencer marketing specifically, we've got a few examples to share:

One of our clients has produced more than a hundred videos on YouTube where each video, made by the creator, is highlighting a specific feature that they really like about the mobile app and how it solves a problem for them.

We recently created and distributed a series of 60-second videos ("Coffee Break Tutorials") for Adobe with a behind-the-scene look at how some of the most talented photographers in the world edit their photos.

In fact, we've produced several campaigns for Adobe centered around the idea that people that follow talented photographers on Instagram are eager to learn how they create their content, taking them behind the scenes of how their photos are made.

Principle 2. Making it easy to talk about

Half the battle is often to encapsulate and simplify an idea to a point where it's easy to talk about from both a content creator and content consumer point of view. Keep it simple, and it will be easy and more likely to talk about. In short, if you can't share the core idea in less than a few sentences around the dinner table, it's likely not going to get passed around among people.

---

[24]www.dove.com/us/en/stories/about-dove/dove-real-beauty-pledge.html

The other benefit of an easy-to-talk-about concept, idea, product, or experience is how it ultimately shortens the viral cycle time. Much has been written about virality so I won't go into great depth on the subject, but "viral cycle time" is essentially the time it takes from the second your message is received by somebody until that person spreads the word to the next person.

The shorter the viral cycle time, the quicker it spreads.

Principle 3. Feel good to share

I recently discovered an article from 1966 in the Harvard Business Review by Ernest Dichter. In the 52-year-old article, titled "How Word-of-Mouth Advertising Works,"[25] the American psychologist and marketing expert, known as the father of motivational research, outlined the findings from his research uncovering that a person is more likely to talk about a brand if he "gets something out of it."

But how does this connect to why we're sharing what feels good to share?

His research revealed that we receive self-satisfaction from spreading what feels good to share specifically from the point of view of confirming our ownership and joy of the product, service, or experience—and more specifically our discovery of it. Think no further than back to a recent experience at a restaurant, concert, or vacation that made you feel really good and how you came back from the experience and immediately told your friends about it. It helped you relive and receive the lovely feeling you felt at that time, and it made the other person feel good, too.

Principle 4. Evoke a sense that the world is an amazing place

There are a lot of negative things in the world—a lot of terrible things happening all the time, lots of problems that need to get solved—but life cannot just be about solving one miserable problem after another. There needs to be things that inspire you, that make you glad to wake up in the morning and be part of humanity...

—Elon Musk[26]

Ideas that successfully evoke the sense that the world is an amazing place—especially brands, services, and products that are doing well—tend to evoke precisely these feelings. This also extends to people on both small and grand scale.

---

[25] http://brandautopsy.com/2013/09/ernest-dichter-on-word-of-mouth-marketing.html
[26] Westworld Panel, SXSW 2018

JFK evoked the sense that the world is an amazing place by declaring that he'd put a man on the moon. Elon Musk walked in his footsteps and have proclaimed that his goal is to build a self-sustaining city on Mars.

The principle of evoking a sense that the world is an amazing place isn't just for those that are going to space—the idea also can also be applied at microscale from both a person, brand, and storytelling perspective. Look no further than, for instance, People Are Awesome[27] on Instagram and you'll see how millions of people engage, relate, and share stories that are built around the fourth principle.

Principle 5. Starting a conversation

The best kind of word of mouth is overheard by the office water cooler, at dinner with friends, or on your morning commute. Topics of conversation that start discussions, provoke debates, and even polarize its audience.

There are countless examples of products, services, and creative advertising campaigns built around the idea of starting a conversation to amplify its earned media and word of mouth—and what came to mind when I thought about this fifth principle was a marketing project that I worked on with my team back in 2016. A rather unusual PR campaign with an element of influencer marketing. The conversation starter and topic of conversation?

"Could a long jump suit made of condom material make athletes perform better?"

The publicity stunt and marketing campaign[28] from SKYN Condoms was perfectly timed with the 2016 Olympics Games. Inspired by the record-breaking high-performance swimsuit from Speedo, famous for how it was developed to mimic sharkskin (and later banned from the Olympics[29]), SKYN set out to tap into a conversation that was already happening.

And while the campaign wasn't promoting their core product or the unique selling points of their condoms, it started a conversation about performance and alternative material design (non-latex products, ideal for people with allergies or sensitivity), right around the time when everyone was talking about the Olympics.

"When an athlete soars into the air, the flaps [on the jumpsuit] open up, creating an upward lift that could help long jumpers stay in the air a little bit longer," he explains to Complex. "The apparel hasn't been formally tested in

---

[27] www.peopleareawesome.com
[28] www.core77.com/posts/56320/Taking-Condoms-Out-of-the-Bedroom-and-Onto-the-Athletic-Track
[29] https://abcnews.go.com/Politics/full-body-swimsuit-now-banned-professional-swimmers/story?id=9437780

labs, but our aerodynamics consultants say that, in theory, SKYNFEEL APPAREL could actually help athletes jump just a little bit further."[30]

Was this a joke? Would it work? Could the apparel be used by athletes in the Olympics? Would such practice even be allowed?

To amplify the conversation across social media, SKYN teamed up with a dozen actors, models, athletes, and TV hosts on Instagram, each sharing videos and photos of the conceptual long jump suit, inviting their audience to share their point of view. The level of engagement and the conversations that took place across hundreds of thousands of consumers that interacted with the campaign was like nothing I had ever seen. The campaign, designed to turn up the discussion around alternative material design, quickly ignited a wildly engaging conversation in its key target audience and successfully started a relevant discussion (and even debate) among the millions of consumers that they reached with their campaign.

Principle 6. Relevance to your core target audience

Sometimes overlooked, what's often more important than having a message or idea that will travel between people is to determine if the message itself is relevant to your core target segment. This isn't revolutionary, but an important reminder for you to align your creative idea with your core target audience.

Principle 7. Exceeding your expectations

When products exceed our expectations, we can't keep our mouths shut.

This is single-handedly the primary reason—from my point of view—as to how Spotify took off back in 2008 in Sweden (and later conquered the world).

It can't be THAT good…Oh… wait…What happened?

Think about a recent conversation you've had with someone that is trusted with your opinion. Someone you influence. Chances are that your recommendation is driven by an experience that was better than you thought it would be. Meeting the expectations of consumers is no longer enough—you have to knock them out of the park. And when you do nail the seventh principle, the growth of your brand, product, or company will explode.

It doesn't matter if it's your local bar, a music-streaming service, free two-day delivery, or a company building rockets that will take us to Mars. Elon Musk keeps exceeding everybody's expectations—but remember that he's playing by the same rules as your local favorite bartender.

---

[30] Said in an interview with David Chaker, senior director of global brand marketing at Ansell (the company that owns SKYN) in *Complex* magazine, July 26, 2016

See, we don't tell our friends about products and services we like. We talk about what's greater than we could possibly imagine.

"Did you see," "have you heard," "you won't believe," "check this out," and "can you imagine" are what will make it to the dinner table. And that's important when 90% of all word of mouth happens offline.[31]

If you can turn your campaign, brand, product, or service (and often just ONE aspect of the aforementioned) into a dinner table topic because it exceeds expectations, you'll see explosive growth through word of mouth. And here's how you do exactly that.

Amplifying a dialog that's already taking place

The key to exceed the expectation of your customers—at its very core—comes down to figuring out exactly what it is that your consumers are saying about you (that their friends in turn are sharing with their friends) and amplify *that* message.

Once you understand *the word-of-mouth loop*, you'll understand the where, how, and why of how you can turn product marketing into word of mouth.

Pepsi Max applied this principle in one of their influencer marketing campaigns in 2017 where each participant shared the surprisingly great combination of Pepsi and Ginger—and how it exceeded their expectations. A bold promise that turned out to resonate well (Principle #7) with those fond of Pepsi Max and the taste of ginger (Principle #6).

Going back to my firsthand experience at Spotify, I'd like to share a method I used to reverse-engineer this seventh principle.

Now, it should be noted that there are certain things I can disclose and others that I can't, but it should come to little surprise that the growth of both a subscription business like Spotify and a game publishing company like King Digital Entertainment isn't exactly random.

What's incredibly powerful though, and what I urge you to do for your brand, product, or service, is to dive into the qualitative and quantitative aspect of what drives word of mouth to understand how it can be applied for either your core product, service, or brand or to the development of a specific campaigns, product launch, repositioning, or when tapping into a new target segment or market.

Back in 2014, for instance, a large proportion of the user growth at Spotify was driven by word of mouth—and while it's possible to track referrals and

---

[31] Ed Keller and Brad Fay, *The Face-to-Face Book: Why Real Relationships Rule in a Digital Marketplace* (Free Press, 2012)

traffic sources, it's even more powerful to ask your users why they bought your product, subscribed to your service, or downloaded your app.

You'll want to go beyond where the users or customers are coming from and understand the how and the why.

How to pinpoint what's driving your organic growth

Get yourself setup with a survey platform like SurveyMonkey[32] or Typeform[33] and send out an email to users or customers that have purchased your product in the last 30 days.

The email should be short and to the point, and answer why you're running the survey and what the benefit it holds for the survey taker (e.g., improve their experience or make it more relevant and aligned with their expectations).

Your first step is to figure out where your customers are coming from. Three examples for the first question:

1.   "What made you sign up for our service?"

2.   "What made you purchase our product?"

3.   "What made you download our app?"

List the most common referral sources and have the survey respondents pick a primary one. A few examples (adjust to fit your product):

1.   I saw an ad for your product.

2.   A friend recommended your product.

3.   I found you on Google.

4.   I read about you in the news.

5.   Other (short-form answer in text).

You'll want to include the fifth option here if this is the first time you're running this kind of survey to learn if there's a referral source you're missing (or phrasing your options in a different way than how they are perceived in the mind of the consumer).

Don't worry though, your goal isn't to build a reliable or scientific attribution model. Your goal is to identify how users perceive their discovery and first experience with your product.

---

[32] www.surveymonkey.com/
[33] www.typeform.com/

Now, what you'll want to do is take all users that picked Option #2 (Friend recommendation) and follow up with questions that will get you to understand the how and the why. Again, you'll ask three questions (phrase them so that they make sense for your specific business):

Remember, these questions are only asked on the condition that the answer to "A friend recommended your product" is true.

1.   What did your friend/friends say that made you buy our product/install our app/visit our store (etc.)?

2.   On a scale of 1–10, how likely are you to recommend our service/product/brand to someone you know?

3.   How would you describe our service to your friends?

What you'll discover when you run this type of survey to your customers is absolutely mind-blowing.

The first question is the most powerful of all, as it will reveal exactly how your product is perceived in the market. You'll have to analyze each response individually and look for recurring themes and keywords. Pay attention to the answers. This can feel like a daunting and time-consuming task...but take the time, and you'll instantly know more about your customers than anyone on the planet.

You'll discover what promises your customers are making to their friends, and by following up with the second question, you'll see if the promise is fulfilled or not. These are the conversations that are taking place around dinner tables, in emails, over coffee, at schools, workplaces, and on the morning commute— whether you like it or not. If you're seeing a large proportion of your growth coming from friend referrals and many of the referrals are expressing that they'd recommend your service to their friends, you're on the right track. The third and final question will help you understand what parts of your service they are impressed by.

You'll also learn that there will be multiple clusters and segments representing different needs, problems, and solutions. This is what I did at Spotify (and more recently for several other clients) to uncover exactly what customers in different segments, age-groups, countries, and cohorts were saying about the service, product, or experience they're selling. Incorporate these commonly occurring themes into your next influencer marketing campaign, and you'll amplify your existing word of mouth. As a bonus, it will help your existing customers distinctly express what you know will resonate with the way they already talk about your brand or services.

Creator-Centric Strategies

Extend your *value beyond pay* and increase your ROI with a creator-centric perspective to influencer marketing

---

Marketing is not a function, it is the whole business seen from the customer's point of view.

—Peter Drucker[1]

Key Questions Why do 9 out of 10 influencers follow brands on social media? What's the number one mistake brands make when creating content on Instagram? What are the ten biggest challenges as an online creator or influencer? What do influencers care about the most when deciding which brands they want to work with? What's the right level of monetary compensation?

Core Principles 1. Value beyond pay. 2. Becoming creator centric. 3. Consistency, creativity, and community. 4. Brand self-assessment. 5. There's no free lunch.

© Aron Levin 2020
A. Levin, *Influencer Marketing for Brands*,
https://doi.org/10.1007/978-1-4842-5503-2_5

I've got good news and bad news. Good news first, shall we? 9 out of 10 influencers and content creators on Instagram follow brands that they like and want to work with. You've got their attention! A scarce currency in the attention economy—where the battle for attention is growing exponentially. Ready for the bad news? Chances are that you're letting them down, big time.

In preparation for writing this book, I spoke with over 200 influencers on Instagram[2] to get their take on the current state of the social media landscape. The research uncovered several relevant insights that can be applied to solve problems and create new opportunities for both creators and brands.

The main thesis throughout this chapter is this: With a creator-centric perspective to influencer marketing, you'll increase *their* value of working with *you*—rather than the other way around. In exchange, you'll create leverage that will improve your return on investment. But what do we mean by *creator-centric*? Simply that each problem, challenge, and opportunity should first be observed through the eyes of the creators and influencers that you're working with. That, when you see things from their frame of reference and embrace their perspective, you'll be fully aware of what it's like to walk in their shoes.

What creators expect

Let's take a deeper look at those good and bad news of ours. The study found that 87% of panelists (each a creator on Instagram with at least 10,000 followers) follow at least one brand on Instagram. That's good news, obviously, *but what do they expect from these businesses and their social media presence?* Following up to the first question, each creator was asked to share both what they expect from these brands[3] and what [from the perspective of the creator] their biggest mistakes are[4]. Examine the 200 different responses to the first question, and four clear themes emerge.

Why do you follow brands on Instagram?

1. Inspiration: I follow them for inspiration (28%), news/trends (10%).

2. Affinity: I like/love the brand and their products (21%).

---

[1] *The Practice of Management* (1954)
[2] The Creator Centric Whitepaper, 2018 by Relatable, 2018. N = 229
[3] "Why do you follow brands on Instagram?" The Creator Centric Whitepaper, 2018 by Relatable, 2018. N = 200
[4] "What's the number one mistake brands make when creating content on Instagram?"

3. Collaboration: I have (16%) or want to (6%) work with them.

4. Discovery: To discover new products from the brand (17%).

So, your brand is followed by influencers that turn to you for *inspiration, news,* and *trends* because they *love your brand* and *products*. They want to *discover what's new*, and either has worked with you or *want to work with you* at some point in the future.

BRAND SELF-ASSESSMENT

Answer these questions before you move onto the next section where we've identified the biggest mistakes brands make on Instagram—and how to live up to the expectations outlined previously.

1. Is your presence on Instagram inspiring with product news and trends from your industry?

2. Is it easy for your followers to discover new products?

3. Are you making it easy for creators to reach out to you?

Next, the same set of respondents were asked a different question. The 200 different answers were organized into 33 different groups, where 80% of responses could be assigned to one of these six themes.

What's the number one mistake brands make when creating content on Instagram?

1. Too product-focused

2. Not consistent or with a clear theme

3. No interaction or answering questions in comments

4. No storytelling, personality, or authenticity

5. Too commercial, transactional and... boring!

6. Your content looks like a magazine ad!

Every other marketing team I share the list with goes *"Ouch! They're talking about us!"* Bad news, indeed. Time for another self-assessment.

BRAND SELF-ASSESSMENT

Answer these questions to assess if your brand is making any of the most common mistakes, according to social media influencers on Instagram.

1. Is your content primarily focused on your product, typically with product close-ups? (Too product confused)

2. Do you have a creative theme that you follow with consistency? (Not consistent or without a clear theme)

3. Do you have a team or person dedicated to answering questions and interact with your followers in comments and DMs? (No interaction or answering questions in comments)

4. Are you telling a story that's entertaining or engaging with personality? (No storytelling, personality, or authenticity)

5. Are you primarily focused on the commercial aspect of your business, and do you use your social media channels to sell products? (Too commercial, transactional, and... boring!)

5. Are you using content that was produced for other marketing channels, like magazines and/or ads? (Your content looks like a magazine ad!)

So, good news—attention. Bad news—unfulfilled expectations. More or less anyway, depending on how you answered the questions in the second self-assessment. Either way, I'd consider these six clear themes your guiding principles to build a social media presence that creators and influencers love.

There's another important lesson hidden within these insights. The feedback is based on the collective experience of hundreds of talented creators, not a single industry expert or social media advisor. These hundreds of influencers, representative of millions of creators, have mastered the art of content production, distribution, and fan engagement. They are, first and foremost, practitioners. They are thriving—in a world where traditional marketing scholars are struggling to keep up—each with their own playbook that keeps evolving as they adapt to the ever-changing digital landscape. And the more time they spend on their content, their tone of voice, and their audience, the more inclined they are to navigate by intuition. The creator community is a tight-knit one. They talk to each other, share advice, and look to their peers for what's coming next.

So, what lessons do they have for other creators, and brands alike, that are looking to produce better content, build a bigger audience, and engage their community?

Consistency, creativity, and community

The panelists were handpicked based on an important criteria: an exceptionally engaged audience—at least 50% above average. In other words, a group of creators that not only have built a large following, but also an audience that is more likely to pay attention to their content.

When asked what their number one piece of advice is to other creators, two suggestions kept resurfacing.

Consistency (or finding your niche) and *engaging with your community.*

Thinking of the list of common mistakes from before, these suggestions appear to be a different side of the same coin. Here's what one creator suggests, on consistency: *"I would advise them to focus on their content and quality more than anything else—at first. People will click on your profile and their first glance will determine if they want to follow you or not, so maintaining an image or a 'brand' will showcase your work a lot more neatly and people will more likely follow you if they 1) know exactly what to expect from you; 2) enjoy the quality and consistency."*

Another common mistake, frequently called out in the research, is the absence of community building. *"Many brands will ask a question to their followers in their caption while ignoring questions their audience ask them. That's a huge mistake and demonstrate that they really don't care,"* one influencer commented.

Now that you've walked a few steps in their shoes, and have a better understanding of what the creative community like and dislike about the brands they follow, it's time to dial things up a notch and uncover what *their* biggest problems are.

Remember our thesis? Increase their value that creators will get from working with your brand, and you'll improve your return on investment. But how do you increase their value—beyond obvious additional monetary compensation? You solve their problems and challenges. And when you do, you're trading something far more valuable than money. In exchange for the value you create, you'll become an invaluable partner.

Value beyond pay

What's your number one challenge as an online content creator/influencer? If you know the answer to this question and can shape your influencer marketing strategy to be centered around solving their problems, you'll win the creative community and consequently unlock an opportunity to turn influencer marketing into your most valuable distribution channel. To save you the trouble, we've interviewed hundreds of creators and influencers over the last few years and identified the following list (in order of relevance).

What's your number one challenge as an online content creator/ influencer?

1. Creating high-quality content

2. Beating the Instagram Algorithm

3. Engage my followers

4. Reach a bigger audience

5. Coming up with new ideas

6. Finding the time

7. Getting collaborations with brands

8. Stand out and be original

9. Create authentic and engaging collaborations

10. Posting frequently (every day)

Observe closely, and two clear themes emerge—*content strategy* (#1, #5, #8, #9) and *audience engagement* (#2, #3, #4, #10). In other words, if you can build a *content strategy* that's centered around helping influencers create high-quality content, dream up new ideas, stand out and be authentic and engaging you'll create something that's far more valuable than just monetary compensation, and as a result, you'll both see greater value in the partnership. Similarly, if you can create a brief or campaign idea that's wildly engaging and, for instance, can drive additional reach through cross-promotion or distribution (*audience engagement*), you're building a strategy centered around pain points that almost everyone can agree are top priorities.

Did you notice that two of the challenges belonged to neither of the themes? *6. Finding the time* and *7. Getting collaborations with brands*. Let's address both.

By following the steps outlined in Chapter 6: 1:1 Relationships at Scale, you'll master the art of efficiency and eliminating constraints—you'll demonstrate proactively that you respect the time and energy of those you seek to work with. The second challenge is obviously fulfilled by collaborating with *your* brand, but there's more. If you can showcase how collaborating with your brand may result in additional partnerships, you'll immediately increase the value of your relationship.

BRAND SELF-ASSESSMENT

Review the list. Rank from 1 to 10 how likely your brand is positioned to solve each challenge—either in general or for a specific campaign brief. What would change the score?

Brand and campaign examples

To put these insights into the context of marketing, you'll now see five different examples of companies that have implemented a creator-centric strategy in their products, brands, and campaigns to increase their value beyond pay.

Sugar Bear Hair

www.sugarbearhair.com

What they do: E-commerce, hair minerals

Marketing challenge: Commodity, no storytelling aspect

Pain points solved: High-quality content, authentic collaborations, coming up with new ideas

Creator-centric strategy: By designing their product in a way that enable participating influencers to be creative with different ways of expressing their affinity for the product, Sugar Bear Hair can tap into a huge pool of creative talent and give them the freedom to come up with new ideas and high-quality content—even though they are centered around their product.

YouTube Music

music.youtube.com

What they do: Premium music-streaming service

Marketing challenge: Saturated market, strong affinity for direct competition

Pain points solved: Stand out and be original, engage my followers, finding the time

Creator-centric strategy: YouTube Music had artists and influencers invite their fans for exclusive launch sessions. This enabled an experience where participants couldn't stop themselves from distributing authentic storytelling and tell others about what was going on.

Adobe

www.adobe.com

What they do: Photo-editing software for photographers

Marketing challenge: Inspire the next generation of photographers to take their photography to their next level

Pain points solved: Reach a bigger audience, engage my followers, stand out and be original, create authentic collaborations

Creator-centric strategy: The audience that follow popular photographers on Instagram all aspire to create their own high-quality content. Also, they all want to follow along behind the scenes and learn how the content from their favorite creators are made. By setting up "behind the scene" webinars where creators invited their followers to show exactly how their most popular photos were made, Adobe was able to not only solve a pain point for their creators, but also for their audience.

Revolve Clothing

www.revolve.com

What they do: E-commerce, clothing and women's wear

Marketing challenge: Saturated market, expensive

Pain points solved: Creating high-quality content, reach a bigger audience

Creator-centric strategy: Revolve in the Hamptons is exactly what it sounds like—a house in an aspirational setting. But it's more than that. It's a creator-centric experience that help the many creators and influencers that they host create high-quality content. With stylists, makeup artists, and a combination of celebrity, fame, and fashion, Revolve has been able to create a setting that helps influencers solve their number one challenge.

Museum of Ice Cream

www.museumoficecream.com

What they do: Museum exhibition and ticket sales

Marketing challenge: Low interest in target audience, saturated market

Pain points solved: Creating high-quality content, stand out and be original, coming up with new ideas

Creator-centric strategy: Museum of Ice Cream is built for Instagram. Unlike a traditional museum, each part of the exhibition is set up in a way that invites its visitors to craft creative, high-quality content. With their tickets in more demand than supply, Museum of Ice Cream has created a setting that enables its visitors (and influencers) to create unique content and stories.

What creators want: Determining factors for brand partnerships

Several pieces of the creator-centric puzzle are beginning to fall into place. In this section, we'll be digging into another important aspect of the creator-centric approach to influencer marketing, namely, what creators expect and are looking for…from your brand! *Getting collaborations with brands* came in at number seven on the list of common challenges among influencers—but it turns out that it's not just any collaboration, from any brand. In an interview series[5] from 2017, we interviewed 81 influential social media creators to understand how many brands that they are approached by each month. The outcome? Between 10 and 100 proposals per month or 20 on average. Clearly, there's no shortage of opportunities. Yet most of these brand inquiries go unanswered. But why?

Values and personal brand alignment

Brand safety, and assuring that *your* branded content is displayed in a risk-averse contextually appropriate environment, is a commonly cited concern among marketers that practice influencer marketing. As such, brands right-fully invest both time and resources to assure that they team up with the right individuals.

But be aware that the door swings both ways, and *personal brand alignment* is actually the number one deciding factor when influencers decide to partner, or not partner, with your brand[6]. See Figure 5-1.

The Creator Centric Whitepaper, 2018 by Relatable, 2018. N = 200
[5] Creator interview series from 2017: "Behind The Feed," Relatable. N=81
[6] "Influencer Survey by AspireIQ," November 2018. N = 200

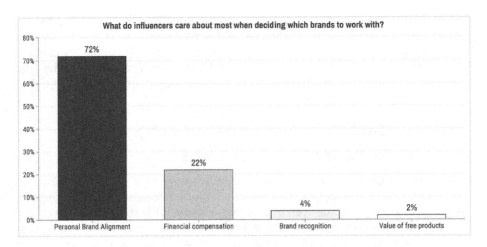

Figure 5-1. What do influencers care about most when deciding which brands to work with?[7]

The study from influencer marketing firm AspireIQ found, surveying 200 influencers on their platform, that personal brand alignment (72% of respondents) was more important than financial compensation, brand recognition, and the value of free products combined. This insight is mirrored by the 2020 Influencer Wellness Report[8] published by my own company—where we found *aligned core values* to be the number one deciding factor on deciding to partner with a brand. See Table 5-1.

Table 5-1. Deciding factors, brand collaboration

Factor	Respondents
How much they pay	14%
That I know their product/service works	27%
That I have heard of their brand before	3%
That their core values are aligned with mine	34%
That they give me creative freedom	23%

Independent of each other, both studies reveal another interesting insight: *Your brand values are more important than how well known you are.* Just 4% in the survey by AspireIQ and 3% in the 2020 Influencer Wellness Report. This is great news

---

[7] "Influencer Survey by AspireIQ," November 2018. N = 200
[8] www.relatable.me/wellness-trends-2020

for smaller direct-to-consumer start-ups or brands with low unaided awareness—as long as you can communicate what you stand for and why.

The only deciding factor to rank lower than brand recognition? The value of your free products.

There's no such thing as a free lunch

In 2020, the global advertising spend in the influencer marketing industry is estimated to be somewhere between 5 and 10 billion dollars[9] and is expected to approach over 20 billion dollars no later than 2024.[10] People are turning into media companies, and marketing teams are allocating dedicated advertising budgets to work with creators and influencers to reach their marketing goals.

Clearly, marketers have the value of investing in influencer marketing. Yet unrealistically, low monetary compensation is frequently cited as a turnoff by creators on both Instagram and YouTube. What's going on?

First, certain brands simply believe that free products are enough to compensate creators for their work. There's nothing inherently wrong with giving away products or services for promotional purposes. In fact, it's been common practice since long before social media first saw the light of day and can be effective PR strategy to earn free publicity. But it should, in my opinion, be considered nothing more than that exactly that, earned media.

The digital and traditional media publishing business works the same way. Got a newsworthy story about your product or brand and you *could* be rewarded with free exposure, good, or bad. Advertise, and you'll trade media dollars for predetermined reach and frequency. But note that neither practice is paid for with your product. So why is influencer marketing still believed, by some, to be an exception to this rule? Ethics aside (generally a dangerous presupposition, but relevant in this context), compensating creators on YouTube and Instagram with nothing but the perceived value of your product can be derived from the fact that it once proved to be an effective, and accepted, practice. But those days are long gone.

And note that although the Fair Labor Standards Act (inclusive of minimum wage requirements) has been around since 1938, there's no regulatory compliance that inherently prohibits your company from exchanging your product for social media collaborations. But there are practical implications.

---

[9] https://mediakix.com/blog/influencer-marketing-industry-ad-spend-chart/
[10] www.marketsandmarkets.com/Market-Reports/influencer-marketing-platform-market-294138.html

Ever heard the expression "if you pay peanuts, you get monkeys"? The idiom suggests that if you pay very low wages, you'll only attract incompetent or unskilled workers (because better works can go elsewhere to earn better wages). The same is true when you build your influencer marketing strategies.

As seen in the research from AspireIQ, financial compensation ranked 10x higher than the value of free products (22% vs. 2%). As such, the perceived value of your products is generally very low. Internal research within our company, based on over 10,000 collaborations across Instagram and YouTube, including interviews and surveys to thousands of influencers, further suggests that only 8% responds positively to collaborations where the sole compensation is free products. The practical implications of compensating influencers with nothing but your product is that you'll work 10x more to accomplish the same results.

Clearly, little to no value is assigned to product giveaways, but how do creators decide on the right level of financial compensation and *their* value? Gathering data from 839 influencers across YouTube and Instagram, between 2018 and 2019, suggests that the most common determining factor is *"the size of my audience and what the brand is asking me to do."*[11] So how much are creators looking to get paid, then?

Industry rates

In recent years, the influencer marketing landscape has evolved dramatically, and there's nothing indicating that the growth trajectory of the industry will slow down either. These rapid developments had led to ever-changing formats, best practices, and industry rates.

It's the very nature of the media publishing industry—which has always been dictated by a virtuous cycle of supply and demand. Initially, there's advertising inventory in abundance. Because of the excess in supply, and lack of demand, it's inexpensive to advertise. Almost free. As a result, advertisers flock like geese to leverage the new-found opportunity, and the shortage of supply eventually creates an opportunity for publishers or whomever owns the advertising inventory to charge more. The cost to advertise in digital media differs by quarter, industry, and market. On most platforms and networks, the change is instant, in real time, not to mention new creative formats, targeting capabilities, and advertising technologies.

---

[11] Internal research, Relatable. 2018–2019. N=839 (Multi-choice question: "How do you know what to charge for a collaboration with a brand?")

I'd love to offer a comprehensive influencer marketing rate card that would pass the test of time—but whatever I'd put in writing would likely be outdated by the time you're reading this. What we can do, however, is to clarify what *"the size of my audience and what the brand is asking me to do"* really entails.

Setting aside what you believe to be the right way to media plan and measure the impact of your marketing efforts, when a social media creator reference the size of their audience in the context of a brand deal, it's either *their follow-ers on Instagram* (as opposed to the actual reach their content will get) or *estimated views on YouTube* (as opposed to subscriber count or actual views).

In advertising and influencer marketing alike, *CPM ("cost per mille"*[12]*)* is commonly used to measure and estimate what the brand will pay for 1000 units in their advertising, typically reach, views, or impressions. On Instagram, this unit is *followers*.

Within the creator community on YouTube, *CPV ("cost per view")* is frequently applied to estimate the cost, or value, of a partnership. Here, on the other hand, the number is neither based on channel subscribers (the equivalent of a follower on Instagram) or delivered views (actual impressions or reach), but an estimation of future viewership. That estimate is typically based on the average or median views of the five to ten most recent videos during the first 30 days after publishing date.

Naturally, there will be other key variables across both platforms that will impact the cost per thousand followers or cost per view. On Instagram, this will include content format, workload, content rights, number of posts or stories, and seasonality. For YouTube, the decision to produce *dedicated or integrated videos* (see "Nine proven creative executions on YouTube" in Chapter 4: The Art and Science of Creativity) will impact your cost per view more than anything—where fully dedicated videos will cost anywhere from 1.5× to 3× more than an integrated mention of your product or brand.

NOT TOO LITTLE, NOT TOO MUCH

While compensating *too little* or not at all has practical implications, so does paying *too much*. When you do, you're introduced to another challenge: outcome. You do after all have a limited marketing budget (and a boss with unrealistic expectations for what can be accomplished with those media dollars).

How do you balance the two? Apply the *participation rate* concept outlined in Chapter 6: 1:1 Relationships at Scale and remember that it's perfectly within reason that 15%–25% of influencers accept your terms.

---

[12] *Mille*, Latin for *THOUSAND*

Set clear payment terms

The State of the Brand Deal[13], a research report published by Internet Creators Guild[14] in June 2017, found that 29% of survey respondents have experienced a collaboration with a brand where they've had a hard time getting paid. Every third person—that's crazy! Surprised by the large share of online creators that would attest to this negative experience, we polled a larger pool of social media influencers[15] and came to the same conclusion. Twenty-six percent said that they've done a sponsored collaboration, been promised payment, and then end up not getting paid at all.

The implication is simple: Every third person you reach out has been cheated on their compensation in the past—and if not, are almost guaranteed to know someone that has. So, what's the advice? Set clear payment terms right away, with no room for doubt. You can use the following chart (Figure 5-2) to guide your payment terms and set terms that are aligned with expectations.

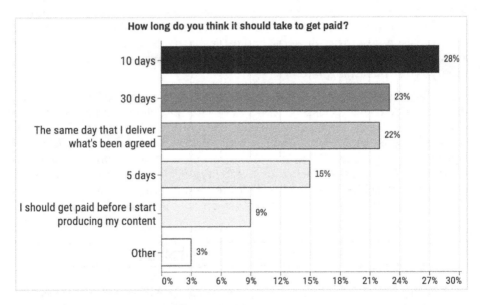

Figure 5-2. How long do you think it should take to get paid?

---

[13] https://medium.com/internet-creators-guild/brand-deal-17e60288ea65
[14] A 501(c)6 non-profit trade association that operates for the benefit of online creators
[15] Internal research, Relatable. 2018–2019. N=839 ("Have you ever done a sponsored collaboration, been promised payment, and then ended up not getting paid at all?")

The survey from CreatorIQ, referenced earlier in this chapter, revealed another valuable insight: What influencers believe the brands they work with care about the most. Content quality came in as the most cited answer (40%), followed by engagement rates (37%), follower count (16%), brand alignment (12%), and audience demographics (6%).

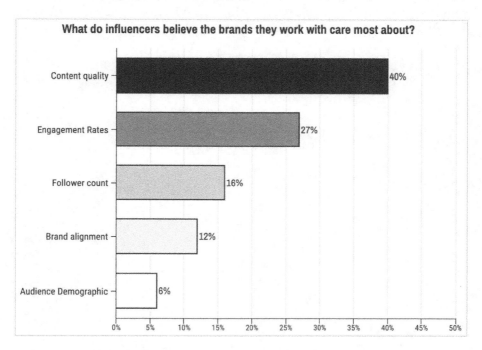

Figure 5-3. What do influencers believe the brands they work with care most about?

While these are all clearly defined goals and important considerations in any influencer marketing campaign, it's important that expectations between creators and brands are aligned—which isn't always the case. Influencer marketing firm Activate came to the same conclusion[16] when surveying both influencers and marketing professionals in parallel to understand how each group perceived the goal of a brand/creator partnership. On the brand side, 78% cited brand awareness as their primary objective, compared to just 37% of creators. Their takeaway offers a great piece of advice for brands and

[16] Activate, "The 2018 State of Influencer Marketing Study," April 2018, https://influence.bloglovin.com/activates-latest-research-the-2018-state-of-influencer-marketing-study-2a6a1a3bcc25

creators alike: *"If influencers have a better understanding of marketers' goals they can better optimize their content to help achieve them."*

The Four-Step Influencer Marketing Framework in Chapter 7: The Four-Step Influencer Marketing Framework will show you exactly how to pick the right marketing objective and definition of success for your campaign. But first, for something equally important when writing an effective creator-centric brief: The Art and Science of Creativity.

1:1 Relationships at Scale

The Theory of Constraints and how to scale your influencer marketing

What you have learned is that the capacity of the plant is equal to the capacity of its bottlenecks.

—Eliyahu M. Goldratt[1]

Key Questions   How do you eliminate bandwidth and time restraints when you scale your influencer marketing? How do you maintain your 1:1 relationships with creators, while reducing 80% of work? How do you turn email communication into your advantage, and not a bottleneck? What is a good benchmark for campaign participation, email delivery, email open, email reply, and click-through rates? How do you build a dynamic model for compensation creators and get rid of unnecessary negotiations? What are the five most valuable third-party software services that will put your influencer marketing on autopilot?

[1] *The Goal: A Process of Ongoing Improvement* (1984)

© Aron Levin 2020
A. Levin, *Influencer Marketing for Brands*,
https://doi.org/10.1007/978-1-4842-5503-2_6

Core Concepts   1. The Theory of Constraints. 2. The 80-20-80-20 strategy. 3. 1:1 relationships at scale. 4. Campaign participation rates. 5. A dynamic model for compensating creators.

When the founder of the largest bookstore in the world recommends a read, it's wise to pay attention. With a trillion dollar market cap[2], Jeff Bezos has built one of the largest and most complex companies on the planet and has come a long way since Amazon was "just" a bookstore. Bezos and his organization has managed to identify the biggest constraints in their operations and built a structure to get the most out of those constraints. The recommended read in question, business novel *The Goal,* was published by Eliyahu Goldratt in 1984 and is considered a bible by the team that built Amazon's fulfillment network.[3]

Theory of Constraints

The book is an introduction to the *Theory of Constraints (TOC)*—a management concept developed by Dr. Goldratt that aims to help companies and managers systematically focus efforts, energy, and attention on the constraints of a system. The constraint is typically a bottleneck that restricts output, preventing the organization to increase the flow of throughput which otherwise would yield better delivery to customers, less firefighting, reduced cycle times, conflicts between team members, additional capacity, or higher net profits.

See where I'm going with this?

TOC's key processes are, in short, focused on removing barriers that prevent each part from working together as an integrated whole. And despite its name, the "Theory of Constraints" is not particularly theoretical. Rather, it helps find practical, effective solutions to challenges within businesses.

This chapter is dedicated to eliminate the many bottlenecks that marketing organizations face when they attempt to scale their influencer marketing. I didn't realize it at the time, but the approach my company has taken over the last couple of years, to help our clients scale their influencer marketing programs, closely resembles several key components within the Theory of Constraints. Especially its mean thesis—that rather than trying to reduce costs, TOC declares that the most powerful and sustainable method for

---

[2] NASDAQ: AMZN, July 11, 2019
[3] www.businessinsider.com.au/jeff-bezos-favorite-business-books-2013-9

increased profit (and return on investment) is to increase your throughput. In Chapter 4: The Art and Science of Creativity, we covered the many aspects of identifying the right influencers for your brand and how to build a talent pool for your brand. Many of the concepts that we've already covered are built on the premise of increased throughput, and in this chapter, I'll pull back the curtain further and show you a set of practical solutions that will help you and your organization knock out the bottlenecks that have been holding you back.

The 80-20-80-20 strategy

A global survey from 2019, across more than 350 participating marketing teams, revealed that bandwidth and time restraints are almost as common of a challenge as finding the right influencers.[4] Further, the same survey respondents expressed issues with both "managing contracts and deadlines" and "processing payments to influencers." Ask any marketer with even the slightest of experience within our industry, and you'll hear about their challenges with email communication, contract negotiation, content submission, content approvals, logistics, payments, regulations, payments, tracking links, promo codes, and reporting.

What's worse is that there's another person on the other end, the creator, jumping through the same hoops. It's a frustrating experience for all parties for a simple reason; it doesn't create any *real* value. These things become a means to an end, consuming as much as 80% of your time, leaving you with just 20% of your time to relationship building, creativity, and strategy (Figure 6-1) components that, at the end of the day, will make 100% of the difference.

---

[4] Relatable 2019 State of Influencer Marketing Report (www.relatable.me/the-state-of-influencer-marketing-2019)

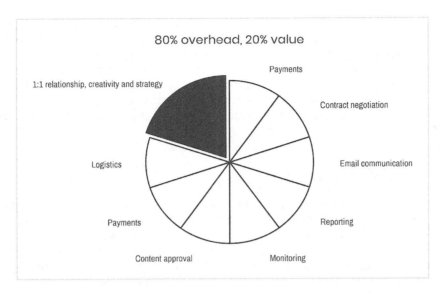

Figure 6-1. 80% overhead, 20% value

On the other hand, as time consuming and frustrating it may be, most marketing teams that are successful with their influencer marketing efforts have all seen the importance of building one-to-one relationships with the creators and influencers that they're working with. It moves the value beyond being pure transactional and allows for you to be more creative and strategic. It would seem like the very thing essential to their success is also what's holding them back. So, how do you increase your throughput (scale your influencer marketing with efficiency) when your constraint (building one-to-one relationships) is critical to your success? And the answer is you don't. You get rid of everything else.

Instead of spending 20% of your time on creating value and 80% on overhead, you're getting yourself a position where you spend 80% of your time on the things that create value and 20% on the overhead (Figure 6-2). But how? Through workflows, technology, and system thinking. With the mindset of a savvy engineer, and a dash of inspiration from the Theory of Constraints, I'll walk you through the shift you need to make to eliminate a tremendous amount of overhead, permanently. And know this—everything you're about to learn has been thoroughly implemented and tested across thousands of collaborations, across hundreds of different brands, over the last 3 years. As such, I'm confident that the advice and suggestions not only works in theory, but more importantly in practice.

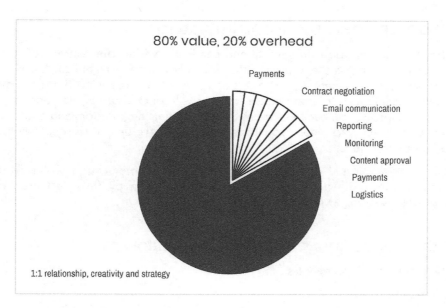

Figure 6-2. 80% value, 20% overhead

The best part? You'll write zero lines of code, and should you happen to hold a PhD in mathematics or computer science, I'm afraid it'll be of little use.

1:1 relationships at scale, with 80% less work

The end goal is threefold: *First*, reduce the time you have to spend on factors that contribute little or no value, as outlined in the preceding text. *Second*, use the time and resources toward relationship building (and consequently strategy and creativity). I'll stress this—the goal is to increase the amount of time you spend on the factors that create the most value. *Third*, build systems (again, no coding or PhD required) that can allow for you to scale your throughput by 10 or even 100 times from where you are today. If you're just starting out, I understand that the thought of running an influencer marketing program with 100 creators simultaneously may seem very distant, but know this: Your constraints (80% overhead) are best eliminated from day one. We follow the very same process, and operate within the same system, to run an influencer marketing program with 5, 50, or 500 participants, and it all thanks to an approach we implemented years ago where workflows, technology, and system thinking were integral to our operations and execution. Because of this, 97 of 100 polled influencers highly recommend working with us and the brands we represent and frequently cite that it's been the most smooth and pleasant experience they've ever had when collaborating with a brand.

Constrained by communication

Email communication (in general and particular within the context of influencer marketing) is a real-time suck. Not only when you're building your talent pool (as per Chapter 4: The Art and Science of Creativity) but especially since it's a platform of communication that will touch most of the constraints that are holding you back—from outreach, briefing, negotiation, and onboarding. Luckily, it's also where you'll see high impact (return) with relatively low effort (investment).

Good old-fashioned email is also a method of communication preferred by creators and influencers regardless of social media platform, country, or industry—as long as it's used effectively.

Step 1: Set up a dedicated email address

Time required: 5–10 minutes

Effort: Low

Impact: N/A (but an essential first step)

The very first thing you need to do (to optimize the rest of the steps outlined in this chapter) is setting up a dedicated email address used only for communication with influencers. As easy and obvious as this may seem, it's essential that you address this before moving on. A chain is, after all, no stronger than its weakest link.

The email address should be from an actual person within your company that is responsible for communication, and it's important that it's used only for that purpose. My work email address is aron@relatable.me (say hello!), so I'd set up an additional one with another alias, like aron.levin@relatable.me (not my primary inbox!). You'll see better open rates, click-through rates, and reply rates if you use a real name instead of an impersonal alias like hello@ yourcompany.com or collaborations@yourcompany.com. Set up the *name* of the account to be your full name, and don't forget to upload a profile picture.

DO PEOPLE EVEN READ EMAILS?

Based on a dataset on emails sent to more than 100,000 influencers and content creators, I can assure you that it's a very effective form of communication if used properly. The following benchmarks can help you check if you're hitting the right notes.

Delivery rate: 95%>

Open rates: 50%–70%>

Reply rate or click-through: 5%–30%

Further down the road, if you're building a larger team or other aspects of your campaign delivery become a constraint, you'll be able to replicate this step and add multiple people to your team, all following the same process—but let's leave it at that for now.

Once you've completed this step, you've successfully established a single point of contact, a focal point of information, and are ready to move on to address the next constraint: the inbox itself.

Step 2: Kill your inbox

Time required: 30–60 minutes

Effort: Mid

Impact: High

Once you have your dedicated email address in place, it's time to kick things up a notch. I'd grade the following action as mid-effort, high impact. Our goal? To eliminate the entire idea of an inbox and different email threads—implementing an approach that's already widely adopted across most businesses.

Now, I can't say with certainty how things are set up within your organization, but it's very likely that you have some kind of support function for your customers, especially if you're a consumer brand. If you don't, that's not a problem—just play along for now. When an email is sent to a support@ yourcompany.com, it's probably routed to some kind of customer service platform, rather than a regular email inbox. This is at least the case for most larger businesses that frequently interact with their customers. Again, there's no need to worry if your company is an exception to the rule.

Either way, the approach holds several benefits: Communication with each customer is neatly organized; they're able to track previous communication and what's been said and connect your profile (in this instance your email address or a unique identifier) to their CRM.[5] If there are several members within the customer service team, they can open and close tickets and jump into a conversation if one specific team member is unavailable and there's an urgent need to resolve the task. This is what *Step 2: Kill your inbox* is about: Implement a similar workflow, used specifically for managing the communication of your influencer marketing campaigns. You'll run your communication

---

[5] Customer Relationship Management System

as efficiently as a customer service team that manages hundreds or even thousands of messages in parallel—but here's the beautiful part: On the other end, from the point of view of the individual you're communicating with, it'll be a personalized one-to-one conversation.

To accomplish this, you'll need a third-party software-as-a-service platform. My company use Intercom[6], and their service will cover your initial needs for something like $30–$40 per month. There's likely a free trial available that you can take advantage of to experiment with your new workflow. Zendesk is another industry leader, although I haven't had the firsthand experience to implement or try their platform. Avoid, at all costs, from using any existing systems or platforms that your company has in place, since your needs (and use case) will be very different from your customer service departments. Because of my experience with Intercom, I'll use their service to walk you through these steps.[7] Once implemented, you'll have this in place:

1. When someone sends an email to, or replies to an email sent from, jane.doe@yourcompany.com (your new unique email address used nowhere else), the email is automatically forwarded to your Intercom inbox.

2. Rather than logging into your email inbox, you'll receive a new message within their web-based client (there's also a mobile app). The interface is similar to Facebook Messenger and very easy to use.

3. Replying to an inbox message is just as easy as sending a chat message. In my experience, it's also a lot faster, because you're given full context from previous conversations and the interface is better organized. You have the option to close conversations, assign them to other colleagues, and even route messages to different team members depending on their context.

But what's the experience like for the other party, the influencer, or creator that you're in communication with? Will they have to jump through hoops and feel like they're routed through a customer service platform? Quite the opposite. The communication feels just like a regular email thread, but since the system allows for you to reply faster and with greater accuracy, you'll be perceived as more responsive and even easier to work with. Time spent on overhead? Reduced. 1:1 relationship? Improved.

---

[6] www.intercom.com

[7] Highly recommended, but I encourage you to do your own research before making a decision.

Step 3: What the FAQ do you want?

Time required: A couple of hours

Effort: Mid

Impact: Mid to high

With a dedicated platform in place for handling negotiations, discussions, and general communication with influencers that you reach out to (and those that you're actively working with), you've engineered a system where throughput of communication, or the number of creators you're working with, doesn't create additional bottlenecks. An ongoing conversation with 1, 10, or 100 individuals in parallel follows the same process, and a cluttered inbox is no longer the weakest link in your chain. Dr. Eliyahu Goldratt would have been proud. But we're not done yet.

Speaking of ongoing dialog, the third thing you're going to do is reduce the number of messages that you send and receive to each person.

First, we need to debunk a common myth among marketers, that is, people don't read, or prefer, long-form content, especially email. I disagree with the entire premise. It depends entirely on what the content is—and if it's relevant to its reader. And know this—most creators and influencers are utterly frustrated with agencies, brands, and marketers that can't give them enough information and are left wondering: *What the heck do you want?*

The following questions, as seen in Chapter 4: The Art and Science of Creativity, will inevitably run through the mind of anyone you seek to engage in any collaboration, partnership, talent pool, or ambassador program of any shape or form (in no particular order):

1. Who are you and your company? (introduction)
2. What does your company, product, or service do? (background)
3. Why are you reaching out to me? (context)
4. What is expected of me? (brief)
5. When is it expected? (commitment)
6. How will we be working together? (process)
7. How much will I get paid? (compensation)
8. What do you want me to do next? (call to action)

Further, if you can answer the preceding questions, you'll face follow-up questions, such as (again, in no particular order)

9. How will this help me create content for my audience? (benefits)

10. Any chance that this could hurt my career or personal brand? (risks)

11. Are there other benefits for me that I should know? (benefits)

12. How do I know that I can trust you? (risk)

13. Who else have you worked with? (social proof and community)

14. How much time will this take? (commitment)

15. When will I get paid? (terms)

16. What are your marketing goals? (objective)

17. What makes your product/service special? (unique selling points)

All perfectly reasonable questions, relevant to anyone deciding if what you're proposing is interesting or not. Your end goal: To minimize asynchronous conversation by addressing and answering as many questions as possible, up front, that is, before the other party even decides if they want to work with you. And when you do, three things will happen: *First*, there's a reduced dialog between both parties. *Second*, because there's less dialog, your cycle time improves. Instead of multiple messages back and forth before you have addressed each relevant question (and likely hours, if not days, of calendar time), things can move forward in an instant. *Third*, because of the clear communication, your relationship with the other party skyrockets.

There could be other frequently asked questions specific to your brief, campaign, or even product that should be addressed as well, but you might be better off addressing those further down the road when you begin to spot a pattern.

Step 4: Cash rules everything around me

Time required: A couple of hours

Effort: Mid

Impact: Mid

"How much will I get paid?"

Negotiating compensation and how much someone will get paid is the only questions outlined in the previous section that doesn't have a static answer. Here, the recommendation is to establish a compensation rate dynamic to follower count, average video views, level of engagement, or other relevant KPIs[8] or marketing goals. Let's illustrate with four different examples:

Note These are entirely made up examples and do not constitute a recommendation on how much you should compensate someone.

Example 1

Output: A set of photos and stories on Instagram

Dynamic model: $30 per 1,000 followers

Formula: [Follower count]/1000 x $30

Creator A with 100,000 followers. Budget: $3,000

Creator B with 50,000 followers. Budget: $1,500

In this example, you'll see that the pricing model is dynamic, with a very simple model in place. Not the most sophisticated compensation structure, but a simple example that remove the need for guesswork. More importantly, you now have a mathematical formula (fifth grade math or so, no PhD required!) in place that you can run across hundreds of influencers that you're seeking to engage.

Let's review a slightly different example:

Example 2

Output: A set of photos and stories on Instagram, attend launch event with a +1

Dynamic model: $20 per 1,000 followers and flat fee of $250

Formula: ([Follower count]/1000 x $20) + $250

Creator A with 100,000 followers. Budget: $2,250

Creator B with 50,000 followers. Budget: $1,250

Creator C with 10,000 followers. Budget: $450

---

[8] Key performance indicators

In this example, you've simply included an additional flat fee, but lowered the dynamic rate. Why would you do that? Because, in this example, you probably have to. Look at Creator C in the example. The flat fee assures that the absolute compensation is reasonable even for someone with a smaller following. You can also build your compensation on engagement and interaction rates, as follows:

Example 3

Output: A feed post on Instagram, optimized for engagement

Dynamic model: $0.30 per engagement on recent posts

Formula: [Average engagement x follower count] x $0.45

Creator A with 3% engagement and 100,000 followers (3,000 estimated interactions.). Budget: $1,350

Creator B with 5% engagement and 50,000 followers (2,500 estimated interactions.). Budget: $1,125

Is one model better than another? It depends entirely on what your campaign objective is. Let's look at a fourth and final example on YouTube.

Example 4

Output: A video on YouTube promoting your product

Dynamic model: $150[9] per 1,000 views, calculated on average view count on most recent videos

Formula: [Average video views]/1000 x $150

Minimum compensation: $2,000

Maximum compensation: $6,000

Creator A with 30,000 average views per video. Budget: $4,500

Creator B with 50,000 average views per video. Budget: $6,000∗

Creator C with 10,000 average views per video. Budget: $2,000∗

In this example, note the minimum and maximum compensation. Why would we do this? You don't have to, but it's a way to mitigate for risk on both ends. On the lower side, we know that too low of an absolute compensation (minimum) isn't attractive. Someone that will spend a week shooting a video for you will demand a certain *base pay* for their efforts. On the other end of the spectrum, your internal objectives might be to certain total number of videos, which wouldn't be possible if each individual creator received too much

---

[9] This is an entirely made up example and doesn't constitute a recommendation on how much you should compensate someone.

compensation. Again, you don't have to structure your compensation this way, but I've included the examples to demonstrate that you can be more sophisticated if you want.

It should be noted that this is something you do internally. There isn't a need for you to communicate the model you use to anyone. Just state what your budget suggestion is.

Obviously, your overall budget and average industry rates will also play an essential role in how much your compensate someone you work with.[10] A rate card or formula for how you compensate the talent you engage in your campaigns will be an essential cornerstone to mitigate the need to negotiate from scratch in every single engagement and dialog that you create. Plus, compensation will be an important consideration for someone to decide if they want to work with you and, as such, something you'll want to be transparent with up front and as soon as possible.

Suggest a budget, rather than negotiate one. That way, your counterpart can choose to accept or reject your suggestion. Once you have a formula in place, you can build a simple spreadsheet using Numbers, Excel, or Google Sheets that calculates your compensation automatically. Table 6-1 uses Example 1 from earlier.

Table 6-1. A dynamic model for calculating compensation

	A	B	C
1	Instagram	Followers	Compensation
2	CreatorA	100,000	=sum(B2/1000*30)
3	CreatorB	50,000	=sum(B3/1000*30)

As you can see, the line items could be replicated with hundreds or even thousands of lines without additional work on your end.

Not too little, not too much

Just like an employer hiring new members to their staff, you won't attract workers with the right skills if the salary is too low. And while there's certainly a long tail of talent out there (as covered in previous chapters), there's no such thing as unlimited supply. Suggest compensation that is too low, and you'll find that no creator, or influencer, will show interest in working with your brand. On the flipside, it's obviously not wise to pay more than you have to.

---

[10] This section won't cover what those rates are or how to media plan your entire campaign, but rather focus on the shift required to make sure negotiation or discussions around compensation doesn't become a constraint.

So, how do you set yourself up to balance between the two?

Within our agency, we optimize for *campaign participation rate*. Creators will accept or reject a collaboration on other factors than compensation, but this has, over the last few years, turned into a great proxy for us. The formula is simple:

Calculating your participation rate

[Number of creators that accept your offer]/[number of creators you reach out to]

Somewhere around 15%–25% is a good benchmark. Go lower than 15%, and you'll have a constraint. Go beyond 25%, and you're probably paying more than you have to. Remember this table from Chapter 5: Creator-Centric Strategies (from the section "What creators want: Determining factors for brand partnerships").

Table 6-2. Deciding factors, brand collaboration

Factor	Respondents
How much they pay	14%
That I know their product/service works	27%
That I have heard of their brand before	3%
That their core values are aligned with mine	34%
That they give me creative freedom	23%

It's evident that there are other deciding factors that will determine your participation rate—some more important than *how much you pay*. With this in mind, make sure that you've addressed the other factors outlined in this table if you see low participation rates even though you're paying fair rates. The opposite is also true: If your core values are aligned, there's creative freedom, you have demonstrated that you have an amazing product, and you could likely lower your compensation and maintain a decent participation rate.

Step 5: Let's fire up the engines

Time required: A couple of hours

Effort: Mid

Impact: High

It's all been leading up to this moment. We've set up a dedicated email address to create a single point of contact, implemented a system to allow for efficient dialog with multiple individuals in parallel, and addressed common questions to reduce cycle times and build even better 1:1 relationships. You have mathematical formula (fifth grade math) for compensation and rely on participation rates rather than individual negotiation.

If you've skipped any of these steps, your entire workflow will break down as soon as you begin to increase your throughput. That's how the *Theory of Constraints* works—in theory and in practice.

Remember our exercise with the talent pool, from Chapter 4: The Art and Science of Creativity? The act of onboarding a hundred people to a campaign, ambassador program, or talent pool simultaneously may have seemed daunting—but as promised, I'll now guide you through the steps you need to take to get there without breaking a sweat along the way. Just like with the customer service analogy and Intercom, we'll use two tools that already exist (95% chance or so) within your organization: spreadsheets and email marketing. You've probably heard of email service platforms like MailChimp[11], Sendgrid[12] or Drip.[13] I've personally used all three extensively, and I recommend them all. Just like with Intercom, I'd propose that you get a different account, or service, outside of what you use otherwise for communication with customers or other related email marketing initiatives.

Your experience with email marketing platforms such like those mentioned in the preceding text will vary, so certain parts of this step will either seem very basic or very complicated, depending on your experience. Don't worry though—just keep the end goal in mind: The shift we're looking to make is to move you away from reaching out to influencers and creators one by one while building even stronger 1:1 relationships.

For the following steps, you'll need a spreadsheet software such as Numbers, Excel, or Google Sheets and an account with one of the preceding email marketing services. In the following step-by-step instructions, we'll use Google Sheets and MailChimp to set yourself up to reach out to 500 creators with the press of a single button. Note, the numbers could be 50 or 5,000. Same steps, same workflow, no constraints. Ready?

Step 1. Create a table

Start by opening up an empty spreadsheet. Your table will consist of a line, or row, for each creator, and column for each variable we need to include in our email (Table 6-3). There's no limit to the number of columns you can have—but we'll keep it simple and stick with these essential six.

---

[11] www.mailchimp.com
[12] www.sendgrid.com
[13] www.drip.com

Table 6-3. Sample table, creator

Id	Instagram	First Name	Email	Followers	Compensation

For the sake of clarity, I've included a short description of each, in Table 6-4, with an example line.

Table 6-4. Example table with descriptions for each column

Id	Instagram	First Name	Email	Followers	Compensation
A unique numerical identifier, incremental with each new line	The Instagram username of the creator, without any other characters	The first name of the person you're reaching out to	The email address	I've included this to show you how to automatically calculate compensation, using our prior example	How much you'll pay the creator for the collaboration, influencer marketing campaign or program
I	aronlevin	Aron	aron@ relatable.me	20,000	$1,000

Your very first step is to populate this table with creators or influencers you're looking to contact. I've populated Table 6-5 with three fictitious usernames.

Table 6-5. Example of a populated table

Id	Instagram	First Name	Email	Followers	Compensation∗
I	aronlevin	Aron	aron@relatable.me	50,000	$5,000
2	janedoe	Jane	jane@example.com	100,000	$10,000
3	johndoe	John	joe@example.com	75,000	$7,500

> **Note**   Go back to the previous section for an example on how to calculate this automatically. I'm using three fictitious examples in the preceding table for demonstrative purposes.

You can use the same structure to populate the table with hundreds, or even thousands, of lines—each representative of a creator. Most spreadsheet software even have functions and features that will allow you to remove duplicates, validate email addresses, round a number (such as compensation) to the nearest integer, and sort or filter by certain values.

Step 2. Import to your email service provider

Once completed, it's time to export your table (in Google Sheets, you simply head over to main menu, select *file, download,* and *comma-separated values (.csv, current sheet).* Then, head over to your email marketing service provider, and import the file. Each service provider will have a simple tutorial or instructions on how to do this. Directionally though, there should be an import contacts/audience or list feature. MailChimp call them *audiences.*

When you import your table of contacts, you'll have to map each column to a variable within the email marketing platform. MailChimp call these variables Audience fields and *|MERGE|* tags. *Audience fields* or *Merge tags* are variables associated and values with each contact (each *an influencer or creator*). When you import your table, make sure that you assign each column (e.g., followers) to a corresponding Audience field with the same, or similar, name. We'll be using these fields to personalize our email communication in the next step.

Step 3. Create and send your email

Remember the columns from our spreadsheet and the audience fields? These will now be put to good and effective use. The final step is to write your outreach email. Previous sections have covered both the questions you need to address in your first email and how to structure an effective brief. As such, this section will only include a short example to demonstrate the use of these variables.

> From: Your First And Last Name
> To: @*|INSTAGRAM|*
> Subject: Instagram collaboration with @*|INSTAGRAM|*
>
> Hi *|NAME|*,
>
> We're such and such and are reaching out because of so and so. Would you be interested in a collaboration on @*|INSTAGRAM|* and @ourbrand? You'd be asked to do this and that, and your compensation is *|PAY|*.

Hit reply if you're in, and I'll share some more details about the project. I'm available on email and 555-123 if you have any questions.

Thank you,
Your Name

Many email services offer a preview function that will allow for you to toggle between your contacts and verify that your email looks good and that all variables are accurately in place. When you're ready, schedule your email to be sent immediately or on a date and time of your preference. And because you've followed the previous steps, each reply to your outreach is sent to Intercom (or similar equivalent).

IMPORTANT EMAIL CONSIDERATIONS

You may wish to consult someone experienced with both transactional and promotional email automation and marketing for the following important and essential steps when you set yourself up with a service such as MailChimp.

1. Verify your domain name. This will guarantee that your emails aren't flagged as spam or appear to be sent from an email marketing service.´

2. Remove all HTML formatting and strip your email layout to the bare bones. You want your email to look like a regular email and not a marketing newsletter.

3. Set the from and reply-to address to your email address. Note that this should be the unique email address that you set up in the first step of this chapter.

4. Consult with your legal team, or an email marketing expert, to assure that you follow all email marketing regulations. For instance, an unsubscribe or opt-out link may be required—depending on where you live.

You've built a scalable workflow that replicates what was previously an entirely manual process. Ready for the last, and final, improvement to our workflow?

Step 6: Who's coming to your party? Répondez, s'il vous plaît![14]

Time required: A couple of hours

Effort: Mid

Impact: Mid

As you implement Steps 1–5, you'll quickly run into a constraint that will limit your throughput. And while this step isn't strictly necessary, it will save you, and the people you work with, a tremendous amount of time. Consider the system we've implemented this far. It has a major flaw that will limit our abilities to scale—a constraint that will hold everything back until it's resolved.

That constraint is *you.*

See, with each creator responding to your initial outreach, you'll soon have issues keeping track of who's in and who's not. Initially, it won't be a problem—but our goal is to eliminate the roadblocks that will arise further down the road, ahead of time. We need to clear the road to keep the engine running at full capacity, at all times. There are, after all, budgets, timelines, and marketing objectives to be met. To eliminate this constraint, we'll use yet another proven method. This time though, it's one from outside of office hours: It's party time!

If you're hosting a party, it's essential to keep track of who's planning to attend the festivities, especially if you're hosting a major event. You could have your guests give you a call or send you a text and let you know if they'll make it—but imagine the headache such approach would cause if you've extended your invitation to hundreds of guests. What a mess! Nah, a much better way—and better experience for both parties—would be to send your guests to a website where they can respond with their status of attendance.

Our goal is to have the many creators and influencers that you've invited to your campaign, program, or talent pool, not respond with their status in an email, but rather visit a website where they can let you know if they're in or not.

Répondez, s'il vous plaît

The two steps required to implement this small but meaningful improvement are quite literally as easy as throwing a birthday party. First, we need to build a way to capture responses, and secondly, we need to direct campaign participants to your page.

---

[14] French for "Please respond," or in short *RSVP*

Step 1: Capture responses

While you could certainly build this yourself, there's a range of online services available that will do everything for you—with no design, web development, or web hosting required. I'll be walking you through the steps you need to take using yet another favorite service of mine—Typeform.[15] (Other options include Jotform,[16] Formstack,[17] Wufoo,[18] Formsite,[19] or Google Forms.[20])

Set yourself up with an account. Login to their interface and start from scratch with a new form. There are both help sections, example forms, and tutorials available if you need help. For what we're aiming to accomplish to eliminate constraints, your entire form could consist of just one single checkbox or dropdown field where you respond "Yes" or "No" or RSVP to your initial outreach.

But how do you know who the respondent is if there's nothing but a drop-down menu? Good question! Typeform allows for you to create what they call *hidden fields*. Within these hidden fields, you can pass other relevant variables to the responses you collect, such as their email address, Instagram username, Follower count, or compensation. Remember the *Audience fields* or *Merge tags* from before? If you include those values as hidden fields, you'll know exactly who each respondent is. Rather than including a full tutorial on how to construct your form, I'd recommend the official tutorial from Typeform.[21]

Pro Tip   If you're shipping a physical product to influencers, you can use the very same form to collect their shipping details, along with product preference and size(s).

When your form is ready, you'll have a link that anyone can access to fill out the form. This is the link that you'll include in your initial outreach email. The link will also include a string of characters called "query strings" that will be added to the link.

```
https://relatable1.typeform.com/to/typeformid?id=xxxxx&name=xx
xxx&followers=xxxxx&instagram=xxxxx&compensation=xxxxx
```

---

[15] www.typeform.com
[16] www.jotform.com
[17] www.formstack.com
[18] www.wufoo.com
[19] www.formsite.com
[20] www.google.com/forms
[21] www.typeform.com/help/hidden-fields/

I know that this may seem intimidating to some, at first—a bunch of amper-sands, question marks, and equal signs—but look close and you'll realize that this is far from rocket science. In this example, we are placing five parameters into five distinct hidden fields within the form, namely:

> id=xxxxx
> name=xxxxx
> followers=xxxxx
> instagram=xxxxx
> compensation=xxxxx

Note that xxxxx will be replaced by actual values from each individual respon-dent. Go ahead and grab the unique link to your form, Typeform. We're ready for the second, and final, step. There's just one more thing we have to do.

Step 2: Call to action

Remember our personalized email from Step 5? We'll be giving it a small face lift with some new copy and a dynamic, personalized, link from Typeform. Here's a sample email:

> From: Your First And Last Name
> To: @*|INSTAGRAM|*
> Subject: Instagram collaboration with @*|INSTAGRAM|*
>
> Hi *|NAME|*,
>
> We're such and such and are reaching out because of so and so. Would you be interested in a collaboration on @*|INSTAGRAM|* and @ourbrand? You'd be asked to do this and that, and your compensation is *|PAY|*.
>
> If you'd like to participate, head over to this link and confirm your participation:
>
> **Yes, confirm my participation**
>
> Once you've confirmed your participation, I'll be fol-lowing up with the information you need. I'm available on email and 555-123 if you have any questions.
>
> Thank you,
> Your Name

"Yes, confirm my participation" is a URL that will send the campaign participant to the personalized form. When you set this up, it's important that you replace the xxxxx values with dynamic *|MERGE|* tags, as follows:

```
https://relatable1.typeform.com/to/typeformid?id=*|ID|*&name=*
|NAME|*&followers=*|FOLLOWERS|*&instagram=*|INSTAGRAM|*&compen
sation=*|PAY|*
```

When your actual email is sent, each *|MERGE|* tag will automatically be replaced by a personalized value. Like this:

```
https://relatable1.typeform.com/to/typeformid?id=1&name=Aron&followers=10000
&instagram=aronlevin&compensation=1000
```

These values will then be passed onto corresponding hidden fields in Typeform, and each campaign participation will be stored within their platform. You'll have a bulletproof way to collect, store, and access reliable data, and it's a frictionless incredible experience for the many creators and influencers you engage in your campaigns. But where are responses stored? Within Typeform. From there, it's easy to both export the data and even collect your responses in an external spreadsheet, automatically.

Step 7: Other considerations

Steps 1–6 in this chapter will get you far, but we're barely scratching the surface in regard to what's possible. Once you've implemented the workflow outlined in this chapter, you'll begin to discover other parts of your process that can be automated as well. A few other considerations include the following (though I won't go into detail on each):

- Automate your entire contract process with HelloSign.[22]

- Password protect confidential briefs (including streamlined NDAs) with Docsend.[23]

- Upload assets for approval with Typeform.[24]

- Have influencers RSVP to actual events with Confetti.[25]

- Connect all in the preceding text to Slack, Google Sheets, or any other third party with Zapier.[26]

---

[22] www.hellosign.com
[23] www.docsend.com
[24] www.typeform.com
[25] www.confetti.events
[26] www.zapier.com

This chapter has obviously been written from the point of view of handling this entire process yourself. There are several self-service tools for influencer marketing available as well as agency partners that will handle this entire process from start to finish should you consider that path. Regardless, steps within chapter are useful to demonstrate how to shift your approach from 80% overhead and 20% value to the other way around. Within the company I co-founded, Relatable, we started off (and came very far) by stitching multiple platform services together. In several cases identical to the process outlined in this chapter—while simultaneously writing our own software. Eventually, we had an entire operating system for influencer marketing in place.

One thing is for sure—we would be nowhere near where we are today if it wasn't for system thinking and the *Theory of Constraints*.

The Four-Step Influencer Marketing Framework

A step-by-step framework to a scalable media channel that is fully aligned with your overall marketing plan.

Give me six hours to chop down a tree and I will spend the first four sharpening the ax.

—Unknown

© Aron Levin 2020
A. Levin, *Influencer Marketing for Brands,*
https://doi.org/10.1007/978-1-4842-5503-2_7

Key Questions   How do you define your primary marketing objective? What are the four different marketing objectives for influencer marketing? Why are brands commonly picking the wrong KPIs for their marketing objectives? How do you come up with a strong creative idea for your campaign? How much should you be spending on influencer marketing, and how much does it cost?

Core Principles   1. The Four-Step Influencer Marketing Framework. 2. Conversion is the outcome, not the strategy. 3. S.M.A.R.T. goals. 4. The four campaign types. 5. The disconnect between marketing objectives and KPIs. 6. The seven questions that lead to creativity. 7. The insights-opportunity-idea questionnaire.

The digital media landscape grows more complicated by the hour, and influencer marketing is no exception. There's a need for structure and clarity. Without a framework, and a roadmap, you won't be able to address how influencer marketing fits with your overall marketing strategy. It will hold you back from ramping up your ambitions and get other internal stakeholders aligned with your plans. This is where the Four-Step Influencer Marketing Framework comes into play.

First, you'll identify your primary marketing objective, target audience, and definition of success. *Second,* they'll become input for platform strategy. *Third,* your platform strategy will guide creativity, creators, and content and, *finally,* outline your budget, goals, and media plan. This four-step process will provide the structure you need to turn influencer marketing into a scalable media channel, align stakeholders within your organization, and streamline your campaign planning process.

Step 1: Marketing objective, target audience, and definition of success

The goal in the first step is to answer three questions. *What is your primary marketing objective? Who is your target audience? What is your definition of success?* Let's go over each one.

Question 1: What is your primary marketing objective?

Your objective should be a clearly defined goal, where you outline what you hope to accomplish. Challenge yourself to set an objective that is fully aligned with the overarching business and marketing strategy—and it'll be easier to clarify how your influencer marketing plans align with the overarching goal of your business or long-term marketing strategy.

The 2019 State of Influencer Marketing Report[1] revealed that a full 82% of respondents are currently advertising on Facebook. With that in mind, chances are that you're familiar with the various ways you can configure your advertising campaigns on their platform. As such, the way brands and media buyers set objectives on for their advertising on Facebook can function as a great proxy for influencer marketing. The approach has two clear benefits: There's clear consistency (across a major digital advertising channel and influencer marketing) and familiarity (with similar naming convention between the two).

Here's another important parallel to advertising on Facebook and important piece of advice: *Each campaign should only have one primary objective.* If multiple objectives are needed, plan separate campaigns for each. Use Table 7-1 to pick what your primary influencer marketing campaign objective is.

Table 7-1. Your objective and goals

Objective	Your Goal
Awareness	Brand awareness or reach. Increase people's awareness of your business, brand, product, or service and get in front of as many consumers as possible in your target audience.
Consideration	Encourage people to learn more about you and what you have to offer. Optimize for engagement and video views or spark a dialog with your target audience.
Conversion or action	Encourage people to take a specific action, such as downloading your app, visiting a retail location or website, or buying your product.
Production	Unlike Facebook or other advertising channels, influencer marketing can be used specifically with the goal of creating branded content for your brand.

When you've defined your marketing objective, write it down.

Conversion is the outcome, not the strategy

It will be tempting to pick multiple objectives and reason that each objective is equally important. Equally, it'll be tempting to decide that the end goal is the only thing that matters: the conversion event, revenue, and sales. Unfortunately, "performance marketing" has become synonymous with *conversion*—and it's easy to trap yourself into reasoning that it's the only part of the funnel worth optimizing for.

---

[1] www.relatable.me/the-state-of-influencer-marketing-2019

Here's a different perspective: There's no such thing as *brand* or *performance* marketing. Only marketing with good and bad performance. Awareness, consideration, and then getting the customer to come through the door to buy your product were all imperative to getting the sale.

The objective of the entire marketing function within a business is to drive bottom-line profits (unless, of course, your company is a *nonprofit*), and generating sales should obviously be the outcome of investing dollars into marketing; but it's precisely that: The outcome and result of all the things you did, leading up to the conversion event. Consider The Coca-Cola Company—one of the world's most valuable brands. Their marketing team invests over $4 billion per year in above-the-line advertising,[2] an investment that translates into over $40 billion in annual sales. Their marketing team understands that the acquisition event is the result of the overall marketing strategy. As such, a highly effective marketing effort to drive awareness and consideration is indeed a *performance marketing campaign*. It drives performance of the awareness objective. The outcome is bottom-line profits for the company.

To be clear, there's nothing wrong with an action-oriented marketing objective—just remember that customer acquisition is never the result of an isolated effort but rather the combination of multiple marketing initiatives.

Question 2: Who is your target audience?

With a clearly defined marketing objective in place, it's time to define your target audience. You'll want to list the attributes of your target audience based on demographics, interests, and other relevant values. This isn't the same as defining what kind of creators or influencers you're looking for, but rather who their audience is. See Table 7-2.

---

[2] www.fool.com/investing/2017/08/27/you-wouldnt-believe-the-size-of-coca-colas-adverti.aspx

Table 7-2. Audience Parameters

Audience Parameter	Value (Sample)
Location	United States
Interests and affinities	Fashion and lifestyle
Age range	21–34
Gender	Female
Other	N/A

Question 3: What is your definition of success?

Your definition of success should answer what your campaign key performance indicators (or KPIs) are as they relate to your previously defined *campaign objective*. Ever heard that your goals, or objectives, should be S.M.A.R.T? First coined by George T. Doran in 1981[3], the expression, and the acronym, suggests that your goals should be:

Specific—What, specifically, needs to be done to create business value.

Measureable—Track, quantify, or at least suggest an indicator of progress.

Achievable—The objective is accepted by those responsible to achieve it.

Realistic—State what results can realistically be achieved, given available resources.

Timed—Specify when the result(s) can be achieved.

The S.M.A.R.T mnemonic can be a great reminder for when you shape both your objective and your definition of success. But how do you set *specific* goals for influencer marketing or know what metrics you're supposed to *measure*? How do you align your team and other stakeholders on what's *achievable* and *realistic*, with the right *time* frame?

You use a proven framework, across four different proven influencer marketing campaign types, as shown in Table 7-3.

---

[3] Doran, G. T. (1981). "There's a S.M.A.R.T. way to write management's goals and objectives." Management Review. 70 (11): 35–36

Table 7-3. The four campaign types

Campaign Type	Attention Campaign	Interest Campaign	Action Campaign	Content Campaign
Objective	Awareness	Consideration	Conversion	Production
KPIs	Brand lift, reach, eCPM	Video views, cost per engagement, purchase intent, interest, favorability, sentiment, conversation	Website traffic (organic, direct), installs, sales, cost per acquisition	Quality, engagement, cost per asset vs. traditional production, speed
Primary platform	Instagram	YouTube, Instagram	YouTube, Instagram	Instagram
Unit cost	Audience reach, CPM	Total engagement, cost per engagement, cost per view	Cost per view on YouTube, target cost per acquisition × total budget	Cost per asset

If your primary objective is to increase awareness, you'd measure the impact of your campaign by metrics such as brand lift, total reach, and the effective cost per 1,000 people (eCPM). Your preference of platform would primarily be Instagram, and the cost of your campaign would scale up, or down, by the total audience you attempted to reach (unit cost). If your primary objective was to drive conversion, you'd select the action campaign. The KPIs change, and your goals are set on things like website traffic, cost per acquisition, or total sales.

The four campaign types

Attention campaign

When you're running an influencer marketing attention campaign, your main objective is to create awareness in a new, or existing, target audience. Your strategy? To reach as many relevant consumers as possible, at the lowest possible cost, with the greatest possible impact. To understand the real business impact of a reach campaign, it's recommended, if conditions allow, to measure the metrics that matter with a brand lift study. When you do this, you go beyond impressions, views, or followers to understand what impact the campaign had on perception or behavior throughout the consumer journey—by asking the right questions to target consumers that have been exposed to the campaign.

Typical brand lift sample questions:

> Do consumers recall the campaign?
>
> Are my target consumers more aware of my brand?
>
> Did the campaign move people to consider my brand or product?
>
> Are consumers more favorably aligned with my brand's message/identity?
>
> Are consumers intending to purchase my product?
>
> Are people more interested in my brand/product?

Brand lift studies can be costly, though—and might not be applicable for campaigns with a smaller budget. In this case eCPM,[4] and total reach, could be sufficient—as long as they are compared or benchmarked with similar previous activations. Awareness campaigns are typically suitable when a brand enters a new market or segment or when the general level of aided or unaided awareness in your target segment is low.

Consider the following example and opportunity:

As more consumers strive for wellness-oriented lifestyles, brands within the beverage industry are offering more nonalcoholic products. This is, for obvious reasons, a massive opportunity for the trillion[5] dollar nonalcoholic beverage industry. The bad news? The level of awareness for these products is extremely low. A trend study on alcohol consumption among early adopters from late-2019[6] revealed that consumers that are looking to reduce their alcohol consumption *aren't* considering nonalcoholic cocktails or drink brands primarily because *they don't know what products that are out there* (56%).

This is a prime example of an industry that would benefit from an increased level of awareness.

Interest campaign

In a world where people can watch, read, or listen to whatever they want, whenever they want, anywhere they want, capturing interest is more important than ever before. At this stage of the marketing funnel, your goal is to increase the level of consideration and encourage consumers to learn more about you and what you have to offer. It's time to address how your offering

---

[4] Effective cost per mille or cost per thousand
[5] www.grandviewresearch.com/press-release/global-nonalcoholic-beverage-market
[6] N=2,267 "The 2020 Influencer Wellness Report by Relatable Trends"

meets the needs of the consumer, now that they know who you are. Buyers that are in the consideration face, however, aren't just paying attention to you—but equally to the many other options that are available in the market.

Influencer marketing on Instagram and YouTube can be incredibly effective platforms to capture consumers that are at this stage of the consumer journey—if your campaigns are optimized the right way.

Both context and relevance are essential components to capture the attention of considerate consumers—especially when the content is aligned to passion points. A 2016 study[7] from YouTube showed that contextually matched video advertising has higher brand lift than traditional ads shown to users consuming unmatched content. Mind that... at the current state of consumerism, these brand lift studies are almost redundant. Look no further than your own shopping behavior and your most recent purchase, weather it was a high-or low-intent purchase, and it's more likely than not that social media content on YouTube and Instagram played some kind of role in your decision.

When I bought a new car last year, I spent hours and hours on YouTube watching videos from car dealerships showcasing the ins and outs of the make and model I had in mind. This was, of course, coupled with endless scrolling on Instagram to see photos and comments from people I decided to pay attention to. When I had made my decision, it was a quiet afternoon at the car dealership. Not a single question after the test drive. I had, after all, already made my decision—and there was absolutely nothing that the car salesman could have said that I didn't know. This isn't an anomaly. When leading research firm Kantar TNS spoke with 500 new car buyers, they found that over 55%[8] use online video to help them make their purchase decision.

Action campaign

Action campaigns are focused on driving sales, acquisition, revenue, and conversion. At this stage of the funnel, you're actively targeting consumers that are ready to buy what you're selling—generally with a strong call to action and incentive. Instagram stories and YouTube are effective channels, the latter in particular for organic traffic that accumulate over time. A YouTube video lives for ages, whereas a story on Instagram disappears after 24 hours.

There are two important considerations when you build an influencer marketing where the primary objective is action-oriented: First, to what extent are your target audience aware that your product exists? How many of them are in a stage of consideration, interest, and desire to buy your product?

---

[7] Google TrueView Brand Lift, Global, Q1 2016
[8] 15 TNS/Google Gearshift Study. UK, Base: New car buyers, n = 500

Chances are slim that you'll rush to purchase a product you've never heard of, that you've never even considered...and your customers are no different. When you have an action-oriented marketing objective, you're speaking to consumers that are ready to buy what you're selling.

The second consideration is your call to action and incentive. I'm of the opinion, and experience, that if you want consumers to drop everything they're doing to follow your lead, you better give them a damn good reason. Most would agree, but the reasoning is also loaded with conflict—generally derived from the premise that a generous discount or too strong of a call to action can devalue their brand.

> *"We're not the type of brand that offer... discounts."*

Sure, many of the world's most luxurious brands, like Louis Vuitton, Chanel, Hermès, Gucci, Rolex, and Cartier, wouldn't ever hand out 30% discount code or promotional bundles to new or even existing prospective customers—but neither do they build campaigns with action-oriented objectives. Look no further than at the very same list of popular brands, however, and you'll find companies like Apple, The New York Times, Disney, Spotify, Victoria's Secret, Kate Spade, and Revolve, just to mention a few that, on the other hand, run special offers, promotions, and discount codes to drive their customers to buy their products.

We don't think less of them for their generous discount codes, $0.99 trials, hardware bundles, or Buy 2, Get 1 Free in-store promotions. We like them even more.

Ever heard of *the 40-40-20 rule*? Originally developed by direct marketing expert Ed Mayers in the 1960s, he found that a direct mail campaign's success is 40% attributed to targeting the right audience, 40% having an attractive offer, and 20% on the creative. In other words, an unattractive offer is just as bad as targeting the wrong audience. So what's the bottom line? If the primary goal of your marketing campaign is to drive consumers to take action, be aware that you're speaking to a small group of prospective customers and that they'll need a really good reason to reach for their wallet.

Content campaign

Each of the former campaign objectives are dependent on having influencers create content for their audience—but the actual content production can also be considered your primary objective, independently of awareness, consideration, or conversion targets. Here, the core benefit is to counter traditional production of branded content (either in-house or through a traditional creative agency), which can be both expensive and time consuming. This is the core objective that you'll address when you work with creators to produce content for you brand. The goal? A steady flow of branded content for your social media channels—across paid or owned digital channels.

With this kind of campaign, you're turning influencer marketing into a method for content production, rather than media distribution, which this opens up a unique opportunity. Suddenly, you can optimize for aesthetics, taste and creativity—rather than audience, engagement, or reach.

The disconnect between marketing objectives and KPIs

It is one thing to set objectives and another to measure the outcome and understand the results. In early 2019, my company interviewed 351 marketing teams[9] to get a better sense of what their primary influencer marketing objectives were and how they measured their campaign results. The purpose of the research was twofold: First, to gain better knowledge on why they run influencer marketing campaigns, and secondly how they define their success.

Fifty percent of respondents said that their primary objective for their influencer marketing was awareness or consideration, followed by sales (34%). Content production came in at first place, with 13% of respondents (Figure 7-1).

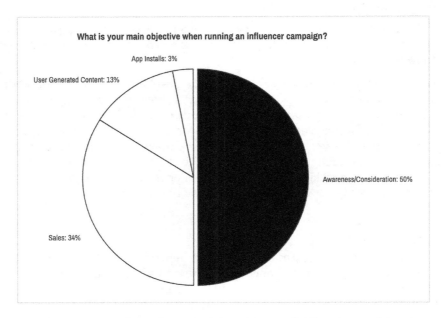

Figure 7-1. What is your main objective when running an influencer campaign?

---

[9] N=351, "The 2019 State of Influencer Marketing by Relatable"

To little surprise, the insights concludes that marketers believe that influencer marketing can be used for awareness, consideration, conversion, and content production—in that order.

Following up to this question, the same respondents were asked how they'd primarily measure the success of their campaign—to get a sense of what their main key performance indicators are and how they relate to their marketing objectives.

Forty-seven percent of respondents said that conversion or sales were their primary way to measure success. This was followed by engagement or clicks (26%), views/reach/impressions (16%), and quality of content (9.5%). But this struck me as odd. See Figure 7-2.

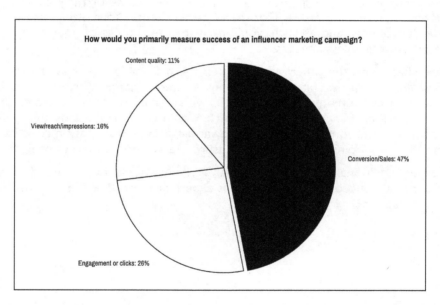

Figure 7-2. How would you primarily measure success of an influencer marketing campaign?

A full 47% would evaluate the success of their influencer marketing based on conversion or sales, while sales itself is only a primary marketing objective for 34% of respondents. This is indicative of a disconnect between objectives and results, and it would seem like the marketing teams we spoke to would aim for one goal and then measure another.

To dig deeper, responses were segmented in two different groups, based on their main objective: *awareness/consideration* in one group and *sales* in the other. See Table 7-4.

Table 7-4. The disconnect between marketing objectives and KPIs

How would you primarily measure success?	What is your main objective when running an influencer campaign?	
	Awareness/consideration	Sales
Conversion/sales	26%	83%
Engagement/clicks	39%	8%
Views/impression	22%	7%
Content quality	13%	2%

As seen in the table, 83% of respondents that claim "sales" to be their main marketing objective will primarily measure the success of their campaigns based on conversions/sales. That makes perfect sense. Your main objective is to sell products, and as such, you'll evaluate the success of your campaign based on your sales numbers.

But what about the other group? When the main objective is *awareness* or *consideration*, the results are suddenly scattered across various ways of measuring the outcome of the campaign, with no individual answer accounting for more than 50% of the responses. It would seem like brands that build influencer marketing campaigns with awareness and consideration goals have very different opinions on how to measure the success of their campaigns.

Through additional comparison and analysis, it became clear that the underlying factor that induced the inconsistency is experience or rather the lack thereof. See Figure 7-3.

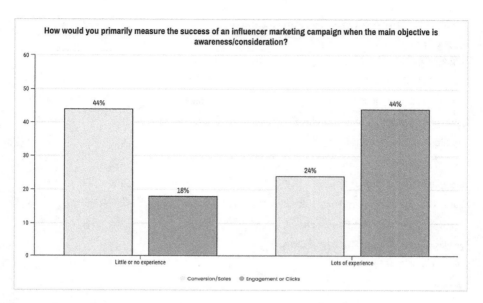

Figure 7-3. Comparing likelihood of disconnect by level of experience

Marketers with an extensive level of experience are more likely to pick "engagement or clicks" as their main way of measuring the results of a campaign when the main objective is awareness/consideration (44%), while the metrics are actually reversed for marketing teams with little to no experience (18%).

With this in mind, assure that your marketing objectives and definition of success are clearly aligned and defined—because, otherwise, there's an overwhelming chance that your own organization will be as scattered as the outcome of our research.

Step 2: The right campaign strategy

Remember the 23 different campaign and creative strategies from Chapter 4: The Art and Science of Creativity? With a clearly defined marketing objective, target audience, and definition of success, it's time to develop your platform strategy.

Consider the overview in Table 7-5 for your convenience (see Chapter 4: The Art and Science of Creativity for more information).

Table 7-5. Campaign types, Instagam and YouTube

Instagram	YouTube
Single Feed Post Campaign	Product Tutorial/Demo
Story-Only Campaign	Product Review
Pairing Feed Posts and Stories	Hauls
Multi-post Campaign (Ambassador Program)	Unboxing
Amplifying Brand Experiences	Lookbook
Burst Campaigns	Memes and Comedy
Real-Time Recruitment	Game Play
Going Live for Maximum Authenticity	Brand/Product Shout-Out
Supporting Hero Brand Campaigns	Favorites
Driving Consideration Through Polls	
Hyper Local Campaigns	
Swipe-Up Lead Generation	
Creating Content for Ads	
Using Influencers as Talent	

By examining the traits of each strategy and comparing their key benefits with the characteristics of the campaign types from the first step in this chapter, you should end up with a list of two to five campaign strategies that will guide the next step within the Four-Step Influencer Marketing Framework.

Step 3: Creativity, creators, and content

Creativity

Things are starting to fall into place and it's time to outline the creative idea for your campaign, program, or activation. This will be the foundation of your messaging, your positioning, and what will be asked of creators and influencers in your brief.

As discussed in Chapter 4: The Art and Science of Creativity, the act of turning new and imaginative ideas into reality really is a form of art. As such, there's no bullet proof formula at hand. Instead, the suggestion is to seek inspiration from others that have deployed successful creative ideas within similar campaign strategies. This is also where creative agencies (or in-house creative teams) can be worth their weight in gold.

With that in mind, the following questions can help spark your creativity and identify a message that resonates with creators, their community, and your customers.

Do you have any unique insights[10] about your target audience or your industry?

What is the opportunity, based on those insights?

What's popular and relevant in culture, right now?

What would connect with your audience at a deeper level and cross-cultural borders?

What would create an emotional connection with the public?

What would have value as a topic of discussion, due to being resonant and meaningful?

What would engage, polarize, provoke, or entertain the audience of the creator?

Finally, you'd have to consider if what you've identified, and what you're proposing, is feasible to produce, and execute, for participating influencers. Summarize the answer to these three questions when you've identified the creative idea for your campaign.

Table 7-6. Insight-opportunity-idea questionnaire

Question	Answer
What is the unique insight?	
What is the opportunity?	
What is the idea?	

Answering all three will help both internal and even external stakeholders see the full picture. Finally, reassure that the creative idea is aligned with the marketing objective, target audience, definition of success, and campaign strategies that you've outlined in Steps 1–2.

Creator selection process and type of content

With a creative idea in place, it's time to find the right talent for your campaign, with the right kind of content. Within the context of the framework, you're only identifying the parameters that will guide campaign execution—and not an actual list of influencers or creators.

---

[10] Including, but not limited to consumer research or industry trend reports

Where will they be based? What are their personality traits like? What values do they share with your brand? What categories are they in? How many pieces of content will each influencer create and post? Will you be working with a smaller number of influencers (each with a larger audience) or the other way around? See Table 7-7.

Table 7-7. Selection process, creator parameters, and values

Creator Parameter	Value
Location	
Category	
Shared values	
Per creator posts or stories	
Total campaign participants	
Average following, or range	

Step 4: Budget, targets, and media planning

You've reached the fourth and final step of the Influencer Marketing Framework. Similar to our previous definition of success, we will now identify the exact targets and key performance indicators that are needed to reach your overarching campaign goals. Your final assignment is to take your overarching goals, KPIs, and unit costs and outline specific project targets. Table 7-3 from Step 1 with the four campaign types (reach, attention, action, content) will help guide what you should measure and how.

Let's start by addressing what will naturally decide the scope of your influencer marketing campaign: budgets.

Budgets

How much should we be spending on influencer marketing, and how much does it cost?

An increasing number of brands, and marketing teams, are allocating dedicated media budgets to influencer marketing. A 2019 survey from Influencer Marketing Hub[11] across 800 marketing agencies and brands found that 86% of survey respondents had a dedicated marketing budget for influencer marketing, a number that was just 37% in 2017. The same research revealed that marketing teams are not only spending more media dollars than ever before on influencer marketing, but that two of three respondents are planning to increase their spend additionally over the next year.

---

[11] https://influencermarketinghub.com/influencer-marketing-2019-benchmark-report/

How much of your total media budget should be allocated to influencer marketing, then? Each organization, and their marketing mix, is different—and it would be irresponsible to suggest a universal generalized budget allocation without a deeper understanding of your unique situation. The same is true if you were to ask how much you should allocate to Facebook, TV, print, out-of-home, or any other media channel. It depends on your overall marketing budget and how much of your budget you're comfortable allocating to the channel every month, quarter, year, or per campaign.

With that in mind, multiple studies across various industries conclude that marketing teams will allocate between 10% and 20% of their overall media budget to influencer marketing in 2019[12,13]. Hopefully, that number can serve as a directional recommendation, albeit a very generic one. Only 11% of marketing teams we've talked to within my company spend more than 30% of their overall marketing budget on influencer marketing, but there are outliers on both ends of the scale. In late-2019 the CEO of Estée Lauder, the multinational skincare and makeup beauty product manufacturer, announced that they spend a full 75% of their marketing budget on digital social media influencers.[14]

With an overall influencer marketing budget in mind, you'll have an easier time allocating the right level of media spend for your next marketing initiative. There's no need to have an entire annual budget approved by your company, but you should operate as if that was the case. Let's say, for simplicity sake, that your total annual media budget is $5,000,000, and you decide to allocate 10% of your budget to influencer marketing.

That's $500,000 over 12 months, or $41,000 per month, not taking into account that your budget allocation will likely mirror seasonality and other key marketing priorities. Note that the monthly number doesn't mean that you should run an influencer marketing campaign every month—although your certainly could. In fact, it's just as common for brands to execute their influencer projects on a per-campaign basis, per quarter, or only in association with new product launches. With six campaign opportunities per year, an annual $500,000 budget would would mean that each campaign budget is around $80,000. That number, or whatever number you come up with for your campaign initiative, will dictate other specific campaign targets.

[12] www.relatable.me/the-state-of-influencer-marketing-2019
[13] https://influencermarketinghub.com/influencer-marketing-2019-benchmark-report/
[14] www.thedrum.com/news/2019/08/20/est-e-lauder-now-spends-huge-portion-its-marketing-budget-influencers

Targets

The different campaign types each hold a set of variables that dictate your campaign targets: each a unit cost. If your objective is *content production*, the unit cost would be *cost per asset*. The cost for each asset dictates how many assets you can produce for your overall budget, and so on. If the campaign objective was *awareness,* and the KPI was *reach*, the unit cost would be CPM— the cost per 1,000 people.

Your goal is to identify a target unit cost that would be valuable for your company—balanced with current market rates, benchmarks, and industry averages. Here's an example in Table 7-8:

Table 7-8. Campaign goals and examples

Campaign Type	Attention Campaign	Interest Campaign	Action Campaign	Content Campaign
Objective	Awareness	Consideration	Conversion	Production
KPIs	Reach	Total engagement	Sales	Quality
Primary platform	Instagram	YouTube, Instagram	YouTube, Instagram	Instagram
Budget	$80,000	$80,000	$80,000	$80,000
Unit cost	$35 CPM	$0.75 cost per engagement	$100 cost per order	$800 cost per asset
Target	2.3 million reach	100,000+ interactions	800 new clients	100 social media-ready assets
Business impact	+10% Brand lift	+25% consideration	$100,000 in sales	-30% production cost

As you can see, I've used the budget and unit cost to identify a target and refined the goals further with a line item that addresses the actual business impact. Does this guarantee and assure that the goals can be met? It depends on how realistic you've been, just like any other media investment. Finally, you can now outline exactly how many influencers you'll use in your campaign, based on these targets, in combination with the values and parameters that you addressed in Step 3. Here's an example in Table 7-9:

Table 7-9. Creator parameters and values

Creator Parameter	Value
Location	United States
Category	Fashion
Shared values	Sustainability, Equality, Eco-Friendly
Per creator posts or stories	2
Total campaign participants	10
Average following, or range	100,000

You may need to revise your assumptions, based on your total budget and unit cost—and that's totally fine. If your target is to reach 2.3 million people, and each campaign participant has 100,000 followers, and each share two posts or stories, you'd need a total pool of 12 campaign participants to reach your goal.

```
2.3 million reach/(100,000 followers x 2 posts) = 11.5 influenc-
ers (rounded to 12).
```

If your goal, on the other hand, was to create engagement, content production, video views, or sales, you'd have a different set of values.

The Four-Step Influencer Marketing Framework cheat sheet

Following the steps outlined in this chapter, and you suddenly have a structured workflow each and every time you're building an influencer marketing campaign. Plan or project. I strongly encourage you to improve and adapt this generalized process to suit the unique needs of your organization. Table 7-10 is a cheat sheet of the four-step framework.

Table 7-10. Four-step framework cheat sheet

Steps	Recap/Summary
Step 1	What's your marketing objective?
	Who's your target audience?
	How do you define success?
	Which of the four proven influencer marketing campaign types will suit your needs?
Step 2	Examine the traits of the 23 different campaign strategies on YouTube and Instagram, and write down a list of 2–5 that suits your marketing objective, target audience, and definition of success
Step 3	**Your creative idea:** What is the unique insight? What is the opportunity? What is the idea?
	Creator selection process: Where will they be based? What are their personality traits like? What values do they share with your brand? What categories are they in? How many pieces of content will each influencer create and post? Will you be working with a smaller number of influencers (each with a larger audience) or the other way around?
Step 4	What's your total budget for this project? Identify your unit cost, target, and business impact using the four campaign types from Step 1.
	Use values and parameters from Step 3: Creator selection process, to identify your overall campaign scope.

Measuring What Matters

The untracked majority, rise of the bots, longevity on YouTube, and how to amplify your efforts with paid media

Not everything that counts can be counted, and not everything that can be counted counts.

—William Bruce Cameron[1]

---

[1] *Informal Sociology* (Random House, 1963)

© Aron Levin 2020
A. Levin, *Influencer Marketing for Brands*,
https://doi.org/10.1007/978-1-4842-5503-2_8

Key Questions How do you measure the organic, untracked, impact of your influencer marketing? Why does influencer marketing on YouTube become cheaper, and not more expensive, over time? How do you deal with fraud, fakes and bots on Instagram? When, why and how do you amplify your organic content with paid advertising?

Core Principles 1. The untracked majority. 2. The longevity of distribution on YouTube. 3. A three-step process for tackling fraud. 4. Amplify organic reach with paid media.

A couple of years ago, I worked with a client in the fitness and nutrition industry. Influencer marketing worked really well for them on YouTube. Their main goal was to create traffic to the App Store and installs for their app. We had sophisticated end-to-end tracking in place to know exactly what happened to someone that watched a video, clicked a link, and installed their app.

But they (and consequently my team and I) had a problem. *We didn't know what the organic uptake from these efforts was.* Like, how many people would watch a video and install the app without clicking any tracking links? A common problem, of course. Across other media channels as well. You'd watch a commercial on TV and buy the product in the store the next week. And as such, attribution modeling (and the cause/effect of advertising) is something that marketers have struggled with since the dawn of time. But if you're investing in a media channel, you'd want to know. Makes a big difference if you get one more customer or five, doesn't it?

That number *will* make, or break, your entire return on investment. To help our client with their challenge, we built a model that looked at normalized average traffic, uptake, correlation to video views, etc., and finally established a number and attribution model we felt comfortable with.

For every install we could directly attribute, we'd get between three and four additional installs organically. That's a multiplier of +300% to +400% in organic uptake. These numbers seemed like they were almost too good to be true. Naturally, I had my doubts. We looked at different markets, dates, cohorts, and videos, but couldn't get to any other conclusion. And as the great fictional detective Sherlock Holmes once said,

When you have eliminated the impossible, whatever remains, however improbable, must be the truth.[2]

The more we thought about it, the more sense it made. Turns out that the answer was right under my nose—and rather obvious. Consumers are less likely to stop in their tracks, interrupt whatever they're watching, and follow a call to action in a video.

[2] Arthur Conan Doyle, *The Sign of Four* (1890)

You're on your phone, watching a video from a creator on YouTube that you like. They recommend a smartphone app, and you'll check it out later rather than abandon what you're watching. Or you're watching the video on your computer, see the app, and pull up your phone to get the app because, well, it's for your phone. In either scenario, the direct attribution would be lost.

But still, when your agency (me in this example) is telling you (the client) that things are four times better than the numbers you see in your dashboard, you better make sure that they're in the right ballpark. Don't get me wrong—I had full confidence in my team and our ability to build these models, *but* the data-sets are limited, and there will always be a margin of error. Not everything that counts can be counted, and neither Facebook, YouTube, or Instagram allows for any third-party tracking on their platforms. In order to have a truly bulletproof attribution model, you'd have to analyze exactly who watched the video and who went to the App Store.

But neither me or my company has access to that data, because I'm not Apple, Google, or Facebook. Thinking about it. Not even Facebook or Apple would have that data because they're not allowed to track user behavior on YouTube. But Google runs both YouTube and the Play Store. They know what we watch and what apps we install. And it just so happens that they've published a whitepaper[3] on how they built their own attribution model for influencer marketing on YouTube to combat our limited tracking capabilities and help marketers transition from assumptions to actual data.

With permission from a select group of app publishers and game developers, the Google Play team analyzed a total of 250 videos with an aggregated total of 60 million views. The study was conducted by looking at anonymized cohorts of signed-in Android users and their journey across YouTube and Google Play, across various segments and game categories—to address the following questions:

Did the users who watched an influencer video actually download the game on Google Play afterward? And is the number possibly higher than the developers used to measure via a tracking link? Or in other words: is there an incremental upside nobody could prove so far?

After investigating the post-watch user journey and comparing the results with the tracking efforts of each developer, the research team found that for every person who is clicking a tracking link of an influencer video on YouTube,

---

[3] Tobias Knoke, "Understanding the full value of influencer marketing for games," Medium, March 11, 2019 https://medium.com/googleplaydev/discover-insights-into-measuring-influencers-on-youtube-and-find-out-about-the-untracked-majority-3403b4a51ad8

there are four more people who are not clicking but still downloading the game within four days after watching. Google call this group of users the "non-tracked majority," and the 4x multiplier interestingly coincides with what we found in a completely different vertical, using a very different (yet accurate) methodology.

Be aware that your share of "non-tracked majority" will differ. 4x sounds good, but it's not a one-size-fits-all (I've seen it differ from 1.2x to 12x), and it's important that you understand your own attribution metrics. Regardless of what *your multiplier is*, you've now seen the huge upside that "the non-tracked majority" will have on your business, specifically, if you're driving installs to an app or sales in e-commerce.

DOWNLOAD FATIGUE

The same study revealed another interesting and relevant insight that is directly applicable for brands that are turning to YouTube to drive sales, app installs, or website visitors. After promoting one influencer video about a mobile game, the second video from the same creator drove up to 3x less downloads than the first one, if being published within 12 months.

This doesn't rule out long-term collaborations or producing multiple videos with the same creators—but it does help predict the outcome of those efforts. Keep in mind that a second video from a creator with exceptional results, even if the results are 3x "worse," could still be better than average. You'll have to be the judge.

Alternatively, a second video could prove to be an effective strategy for other marketing objectives, such as re-engaging an inactive, or lapsed, group of users.

The longevity of distribution on YouTube

While collaborations with creators on YouTube require longer lead times, more work, and bigger up-front investment, the platform offers something that no other paid media channel in the world can counter: unlimited shelf life. When a creator publishes a video featuring your brand on their channel, the cost of that video is generally based on an estimated number of views that the video will accumulate in its first 30 days (see "Industry rates," Chapter 5: Creator-Centric Strategies).

But unlike other means of advertising (and even Instagram where most content gains very little exposure after about a week), the video on YouTube will continue to accumulate views long after its first been published. Day 30 doesn't mark the end of your campaign, but rather the beginning. Consider the following assumptions:

Month 1

Video cost: $10,000

Estimated views, 30 days: 100,000

Estimated cost per view, 30 days: $0.10

You launch the campaign and reach the target estimated views after 30 days, like predicted. But then, something powerful happens—the video continues to accumulate views across search, discovery, and recommendations on YouTube, and the day that video hits 200,000 views, your effective cost per view will be cut in half. That might happen after 60 days, 80 days, or 180 days, but rest assured that the longevity will work for, and not against, you. The closest analogy in the marketing industry would be search engine optimization—where you invest upfront in producing content that yields organic site visits over time, only the difference is that you, unlike with search engine optimization, will see an initial boost as well. Generally, although I should note that the outcome will depend on several factors, you can assume a growth trajectory similar to Table 8-1.

Table 8-1. Month over month growth, YouTube video

Month	MoM Growth	Example Views
1	100%	100,000
2	30%	130,000
3	12%	142,000
4	12%	154,000
5	10%	164,000
6	7%	171,000
7	7%	178,000
8	5%	183,000
9	5%	188,000
10	5%	193,000
11	5%	198,000
12	5%	203,000

Factor in your target customer acquisition costs, average video click-through rates,[4] organic uplift,[5] and website (or in-app) conversion rates, and you have a tool for modeling the outcome of your influencer marketing efforts on

---

[4] 1.5%–5% on average, September 2019, excluding organic uplift
[5] By identifying your *untracked majority*

YouTube. Unlike traditional advertising, the longevity of each video is a new dimension—and unfair advantage—that now allows for you to *leverage time* to improve the return on your marketing investments, battle rising costs to advertise both traditionally and with influencer marketing, or all of the above.

Amplify your influencer marketing with branded content ads

In any given 24-hour period, there's far more content being produced than we could possibly consume in the same amount of time. The supply (of content production) far outweighs the demand (of attention or hours in the day).

In many ways, this is great for consumers, since they get more variety, and the production threshold is higher. It should also, theoretically, not have any economic impact on the producers, whose lower per unit cost should be offset by higher volume. In theory, that is—but in practice, we only have 24 hours in a day, and as such, our demand for content is strictly limited to what we can afford. But consumers are not paying for content with their money, but rather their attention, and suddenly, there's an *attention economy*.

See, if you happened to grow up in the 70s, 80s or 90s, there's a great chance that you remember the very first commercials that you saw on TV. That's not because they were *that* good, but rather because demand (attention) was in excess to supply (content), and we paid generously with our attention. So what happened between then and now? Personal computers, the Internet, and smartphones, of course. According to classic economic theory, an event like that is called a positive supply shock. Technology made production more efficient, thus increasing its output.

The same simple economics theory works on local level, as well. When there's more content than we can consume on social media, companies like Facebook are forced to build algorithms and filters to help sort through the information competing for our attention. Else, social media would lose its relevance, and we'd turn elsewhere.

Instagram is a prime example. With tens of millions of users producing and consuming content, it made sense to show everything, to everyone. With hundreds of millions of users, however, each with a larger number of followers and followings, there was suddenly an excess of content supply, which lead Instagram to redefine how content was consumed on their platform.[6] All the posts would still be there, just in a different order, the announcement read. But double the user base to a billion people, build even better technology for even more efficient production (new storytelling formats, live streaming, face

---

[6] https://instagram.tumblr.com/post/141107034797/160315-news

filters, better smartphone cameras, and faster Internet speeds), and there's another *positive supply shock*. But our demand (attention) isn't growing—which means that you have to grab the attention from somebody else to expand your own audience.

This explains why there's been a decline in organic distribution on platforms like Instagram and Facebook. My bet, based on these basic laws of supply and demand, is that both creators and brands will continue to see a decline in organic reach and distribution in the next few years. Depending on what your marketing goals are, this may or may not pose a challenge that you'll eventually need to address. It has also given birth to a new opportunity for creators and brands.

In 2019, Instagram doubled down on their branded content tools to help businesses expand the reach of their influencer marketing campaigns beyond their original organic reach. By scaling the original feed posts or stories beyond the audience of the creator (targeting specific audiences and measuring the performance using the tools in their ads platform), the approach lets brands, creators, or their influencer marketing partners use campaign content beyond the scope of the original campaign. While similar tactics (with complicated workarounds) have certainly been possible before, the set of platforms and official support from Instagram makes the actual process very smooth. My bet is that by the time you're reading this, there will be even more tools available at your disposal.

I strongly encourage that you make yourself familiar with the official documentation from Instagram,[7] as the step-by-step instructions outlined here might differ by the time you're reading this. Either way, I'll give you a brief overview of the workflow and experience.

First, this strategy requires full collaboration with the creators and influencers you engage for your campaign—and should be a part of your brief. The setup is simple, but nevertheless to be followed step by step to work. Remember though—amplifying their branded feed posts and stories with additional media budget and getting in front of a bigger audience is a good thing where you both win!

Second, when publishing a feed post or story, the creator should use the official branded content tool and tag you as their business partner. For this to work, your brand will need to approve the creator from your account. On publishing their story or post, the creator will also have to select "Allow Business Partner to Promote" for you to promote their post.

---

[7] https://business.instagram.com/a/branded-content-ads

Next, once the creator has tagged your business in a branded content post and given permission to promote it, you just follow these simple steps:

1. Go to Ads Manager and create an ad.

2. Pick one of the available objectives for your branded content.

3. At the Placements step, select either Instagram Feed or Stories.

4. At the Ad level, your branded content will appear in the "Use Existing Post" section. In the Select Post window, navigate to the Branded Content tab. You'll see the list of the branded content posts that a creator has given you permission to promote

Suddenly, you have expanded your influencer marketing efforts to include retargeting, specific audience attributes, advanced frequency settings. You could, should you wish, build an entire paid social strategy that is centered around influencer marketing. Not only that, but you're supporting creators by getting them in front of a bigger audience, with greater engagement, all while beating the algorithm on Instagram. Remember the most frequently cited challenges among creators and influencers? By amplifying their content, you're addressing numbers #2, #3, and #4 on that list—all at the same time.

Frauds, fakes, and rise of the bots

If you're concerned about influencer marketing fraud, you'd not be alone. In fact, 75% of marketing teams and agencies are concerned about fake followers and bots, while only 20% claim to have experienced fraud in their own campaigns. Perhaps inevitable when a media channel gain real foothold with the mainstream—nevertheless a challenge that influencer marketing platforms, agencies, and in-house team will have to deal with to assure that they aren't wasting their money.

In mid-2018, Unilever took stance against influencer fraud, and its Chief Marketing Officer, Keith Weed, declared war on influencers that buy followers and likes on the platform. The declaration made headlines in the press, rightfully so, but advertising fraud has been around as long as the Internet and is estimated to cost advertisers more than $23 billion annually.[8] The social media platforms themselves are cracking down on both bots and fake followers, but what can you do when you build your campaigns to avoid fraud in your campaigns?

---

[8] AD FRAUD 2019: The Economic Cost Of Bad Actors On The Internet, CHEQ

Foremost, it should be noted that an audience of inactive, or bot accounts, may be completely unintentional. If you have a public profile on a platform like Instagram, anyone can hit the follow button. Disregard the connotation that someone has fake, or real, followers, and seek to address your concerns by taking the following actions.

1. The right audience

The audience-first approach to influencer marketing ("Finding the right creators," Chapter 3: Influence Is an Outcome, Not a Profession) is your first action toward assuring that their audience isn't just real, but the right audience. If 80% of their followers are in a country other than where you're marketing, it's beside the point if they are real or not—isn't it?

2. Authentic engagement

Even though the audience is real, there's a chance that the actual engagement (comments and likes) is artificial. But how would you know? Look at the rate likes and comments are distributed over time. Consider the following graph in Figure 8-1, with two real scenarios.

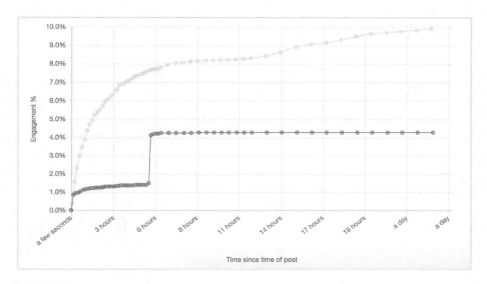

Figure 8-1. Organic engagement vs. fraud

Each line represents the engagement rate on a Instagram Feed Post, from two different creators. After 24 hours, one of the posts has 10% engagement and the other 4%. The usernames have been removed to protect their privacy, but the analysis reveals that one of these has likely inflated their engagement rate artificially. See how the level of engagement flat lines for one of the posts at around 1% only to suddenly jump to 4% in an instant and then remains constant? There's nothing organic about that and indicative of engagement fraud.

3. Beyond vanity metrics

Instagram and YouTube both offer creators and brands account analytics and insights, and it's common practice for brands to either request screenshots or permission to access these insights. If follower audience or engagement rates don't suffice, access to metrics such as feed post reach or story impressions can function as a precautionary measure to battle fraud.

G

Glossary

Above the line (ATL) Above the line marketing includes mass marketing strategies which are largely untargeted and are focused on building the brand.

Accounts Reached Unique accounts who viewed the content.

Activation A marketing initiative to drive users to action through interactions and experiences.

Actual Impressions Rate Impressions divided by total followers.

Affiliate Marketing A marketing agreement between brand and influencer, where the brand pays compensation to the influencer for generating traffic or leads (through affiliate links) to a company's website.

Agency An agency can be either a marketing agency that runs campaigns or a talent management agency that represents influencers.

Algorithm An algorithm is a detailed series of instructions, a computer code for carrying out an operation. It is widely used to determine or manipulate what content users of social media see in their feed and at what frequency. These are often designed based on parameters such as users' historical behavior and patterns of use.

Always On (Program) The campaign is occurring over a longer period of time, not with a single campaign or seasonal-specific timeline.

Ambassador An individual who represents a brand and can be the face of a campaign for a specified duration.

Amplify To drive additional distribution through optimized content.

© Aron Levin 2020
A. Levin, *Influencer Marketing for Brands*,
https://doi.org/10.1007/978-1-4842-5503-2

Audience A group of people and social media users who follow and engage with an influencer. By understanding, sharing authentic, and engaging content, influencers are able to grow their audience and over time build a relationship. An influencer's audience is their most valuable asset.

Audience-First The practice of reverse-engineering the selection of talent based on who their audience is to assure that the right audience is reached in a campaign.

Audience Insights The different characteristics that define the audience of an influencer. These might be age, gender, location, occupation, number of kids, and so on. This information is especially interesting for brands or advertisers who are interested in partnering with influencers whose audience matches their target customers.

Benchmark A point of reference to which things can be measured, to determine success or failure.

Brand Awareness The extent to which consumers are familiar with the distinctive qualities or image of a particular brand: goods or services.

Brief A written document provided to the influencer to clarify the context and requirements of the collaboration with a brand.

Business to Business (B2B) A business that makes commercial transactions with another business.

Business to Consumer (B2C) A business that provides its services and products to general people.

Call to action (CTA) A message that aims to persuade the visitor (viewer, audience member, user) to pursue a certain action. Common examples of influencer CTA's are "like and comment" or "swipe up." The intention is to improve the response rate of the post.

Campaign The tactical execution of a particular marketing strategy.

Caption The piece of text included in a post that describes it. Each social platform has different types of caption parameters: Twitter, for example, allows up to 280 characters, while Instagram's limit is at 2,200.

Click-Through Rate (CTR) The ratio of users who click a certain link to the number of total users who visit the page, post, or advertisement. Influencers who generate high click-through rates usually have highly engaged audiences who take action on the content.

Collaboration The relationship between a brand and an influencer. The influencer produces content for the brand in exchange for compensation.

Content Approval The content produced by the influencers must first be approved by the brand or their partner.

Consideration The extent to which consumers consider your brand for a given purchase occasion.

Content Calendar A tool to plan content.

Content Marketing The strategy of consistently producing high-quality content to engage one's audience.

Conversion The proportion of people viewing an advertisement and ending up making a purchase through the URL associated with the content. Conversion is measured by influencers using tracking links or promo codes.

Cost-per-Acquisition (CPA) The metric that measures the cost of acquiring a customer or new user. Calculated by dividing the total media investment by number of acquisitions. For example, $100,000 media budget/1,000 sales = $100 cost per acquisition.

Cost per Click (CPC) The metric that measures the cost of one customer clicking an advertisement or link and landing on the company's website. For example, $100,000 media budget/100,000 clicks = $1.00 cost per click.

Cost per Engagement (CPE) The cost that is associated with each engagement or interaction, such as a like or comment. The cost per engagement is calculated by dividing the cost of the specific content by the total engagements it generates. For example, $100,000 media budget/200,000 engagements = $0.50 cost per engagement.

Cost per Mille (CPM) or *Cost per Thousand (CPT)* refers to the cost per 1,000 units. The unit is typically followers, video views, impressions, or Gross Reach.

Creator See *Influencer.*

Creator-Centric The practice of building out your influencer marketing strategy with a deep understanding of the challenges faced by the talent you recruit for your campaign (which, in exchange, typically yield a greater value for all parties and maximize return on investment).

Creative Brief A set of ideas that provides direction for content creation. Creative briefs guide influencers to ensure their content meets the brand's standards and is able to generate optimum engagement.

Collaboration In influencer marketing, collaboration takes place when an influencer and a brand work together.

Deliverables The expected results to be produced by the influencers.

Disclosure A visible indicator, such as a written text that is required to clearly state the purpose of the collaboration, the connection between the influencer and the brand. Common indications include words or hashtags such as ad, paid, in collaboration with, or sponsored.

Distribution Channel The platform that is used to share content on.

Earned Media The additional organic distribution generated from the media spend allocated to your marketing campaign.

Earned Media Value The value of the additional organic distribution generated from your campaign with the assumption of a linear media distribution cost. Not to be confused with ROI.

eCommerce The commercial transactions that are conducted electronically. The buying and selling of good or services, primarily on the Internet.

Engagement A term used in social media and influencer marketing to describe the practice of interacting with content.

Engagement Rate A proxy and key metric to determine the quality of an influencers content based on the number of interactions the content generates. The formula is generally total engagement divided by total Gross Reach or Follower Count.

Exclusivity A specific right or restriction a brand or an agency might enact during the collaboration with an influencer.

Flat Lay A photograph, usually taken directly from above to showcase a group of items laid out on a flat surface in a stylish way.

Feed The platform interface where users view the content that is published by the people and influencers that they follow.

Follower Range The term to describe influencers based on how many followers they have. For example, influencers can be categorized in micro- and macro-influencers. Influencer costs are usually based on their follow range.

Full Commercial Content Usage The negotiated and secured terms to the right to use influencer generated content. This means that you have the right to use the content across your channels, but you do not own the content.

Guest Post When a website invites another writer to publish content on their website.

Hashtag (#) A word or phrase preceded by a hash sign (#), used on social media and websites to identify content on a specific topic. They are searchable keywords, for example, #relatable.

Haul *See Unboxing.*

IGTV A standalone vertical video application launched by Instagram. Unlike Instagram, it allows users to upload videos of up to an hour and each user page are named "channels."

Impressions The number of times a specific content is exposed to an audience.

Influencer A creative person or group that has the ability to influence the behavior or opinions of others: The influencer is the individual who may have an effect on the purchase decision in some significant or authoritative way.

Influencer Endorsement The approval for a brand's product or service, integrated into influencers' content in a way that generates awareness for the brand.

Influencer Marketing The practice of connecting influential individuals with the right target audience with relevant brands to help the brand communicate their message to achieve their marketing objective.

Influencer Marketing Platform A tool that helps influencers and brands manage the influencer marketing process.

Influencer Rate Card An outline of an influencer's service costs, which generally reflects the cost of content integrations and sponsored posts.

Influencer Representation Influencers who have agents to help them represent their business interest. Many influencers have management teams and agents (likely to that of celebrities) who manage them with collaborations, deals, and contracts with brands and agencies.

Instagram Business Account The type of Instagram account that provides business with deeper insights of audience behavior and features that allows customers to connect with the business more easily. In order to set up a business account on Instagram, you must connect your Instagram account to a Facebook page.

Instagram Bots Computer software programmed to perform actions such as likes, comments, and follows of other accounts.

Instagram Stories An Instagram feature that allows users to upload a picture or a video on their profile. The content expires after 24 hours, unless highlighted on the account profile page.

Instagram Takeover When an influencer takes responsibility for a brand's Instagram account for a short period of time, to share content with the brand's audience from their perspective.

Integrated When a piece of content is referencing to multiple brands. This type of reference is mostly used on YouTube. For example, an integrated video post, such as a haul mention multiple brands, whereas a dedicated video only mentions a single brand.

Interaction Rate Likes and comments divided by impressions. See *Engagement Rate*.

Key Performance Indicator (KPI) The trackable and quantifiable metric that is used to evaluate the goals of a project. This helps to measure the success and need for activation.

Licensing Acquiring the right to use influencer content based on permissions or usage rights. The process varies in based on the specific permissions a brand requests.

Link in Bio A phrase and call to action (CTA) influencer's use mostly on Instagram to signal to their audience that they have put more information in their bio.

Macro-influencer An *influencer* with a larger following on one or several of their active platforms. On Instagram a macro-influencer usually haves 100,000 followers or more.

Multi-channel Network (MCN) A company or entity that works with multiple channels and content creators, consulting or assisting towards success on streaming video platforms such as YouTube.

Media Kit The digital document, similar to a CV that influencer use when reaching out to brands for collaboration. It contains information about the influencer, previous experience, skills, channels, and followers.

Media Spend The budget invested in a campaign or a marketing initiative. This will typically exclude other costs.

Micro-influencer An *influencer* with a smaller but usually a highly engaged audience (typically 10–100K followers).

Millennials The demographic cohort of individuals born between 1980s and 1990s who have reached young adulthood in the 21st century.

Most Valuable Distribution (MVD) A term used to describe a brands most effective channel strategy and the best practice unique for their brand yielding the greatest return on investment with the lowest effort or energy.

Monetize The process of converting services or assets into a stream of revenue. For influencers, monetization happens when they are able to earn money from created content their social media accounts or blogs. This is often by sponsored content or affiliate revenue.

Multi-tied Approach The activation that strategically leverages various influencers across different audience sizes to ensure all key performance indicators are addressed and high-level brand goals are met.

Niche A small segment in the market of population with unique or very specific characteristics or needs.

Off Brand When content lacks alignment to the value a brand is aiming to achieve.

Organic vs. Paid The two types of influencer content: non-sponsored and sponsored. Organic content is non-sponsored and holds no material connection to a brand. Paid content, or sponsored content, on the contrary is driven in some capacity by a sponsoring brand advertiser.

Optimize To make the best or most effective use. In influencer marketing, optimization refers to making the content perform better.

Organic In influencer marketing, something happens organically when there is interaction without the intervention of payments.

Outreach To reach out to *influencers* for collaborations.

Owned Media Branded content published on a one's own channels.

Page Views The metric used to show how many views a page on a website got during a specified period of time.

Paid Media Any media coverage that has been paid for.

Paid Post A blog or social media post that has been paid for to be produced. Often paid posts are produced by influencers in collaboration with a brand in exchange for a form of compensation, monetary, or other.

Paid Reach Impression that have been earned through a paid model. ROI is often measured by comparing the organic reach and the paid reach.

Personal Brand The personal features, values, and qualities of an influencer. Influencers are mindful to make sure that potential brand partners aligns with or compliment their own personal brand, to ensure authentic content to their audiences.

Participation Rate The share of *influencers* that accept to join your campaign (see *Outreach*).

Plandid A photo that's meant to look candid and casual, but is actually strategically planned out.

Platform A social media channel or website where users post content. Platforms include Instagram, Twitter, YouTube, Snapchat, Music.ly, Facebook, and blogs.

Poll Interaction Rate The share of an audience interacting with the Vote feature in *Instagram Stories*. Votes divided by views.

Product Integration of a brand's specific product through explicitly introducing, including, and mentioning it within influencers' content.

Public Relations The strategic professional communications process that specializes in a favorable media coverage of a brand or personality.

Qualify When evaluating influencers for a specific campaign, some brands may have some prerequisites so a qualification process has to be done.

Reach The total number of followers an influencer or a brand has. This may be on a specific social platform or on all social platforms that are active.

Reaction Video Videos in which people react to events or other videos.

Return on Investment (ROI) The total value received on a marketing investment.

Sampling Goods or services are provided as a form payment for the influencer in a collaboration.

Segment A specific group of influencers differentiated by the type of content they create or by the specific audience demographics they reach. Examples: lifestyle, fashion, parenting, travel, and so on.

Sentiment The opinions expressed by followers.

Sentiment Analysis Computational process to identify opinions expressed by followers within the comments in response to influencer content. This helps to determine attitudes toward a particular topic or product.

Social Media The collective of online communication channels that enable users to create and share content and to participate in social networking.

Swipe up The feature on both Instagram Stories and Snapchat that allows the user to link to a website from their post, so that their audience can get more specific information. The user need to swipe up on the screen to land on the website.

Tag Typically a @tag on a post to link to another user's page on the platform.

Target Audience The ideal group of consumers that a brand wants to attract with a marketing campaign.

Terms of Service (TOS) The terms or rules that have to be agreed upon before using a product or a service.

Through the Line (TTL) 360-degree advertising where campaigns are developed with the vision of brand building as well as conversion.

Total Accounts Reached Total unique accounts that viewed the content.

Total Content Engagement The sum of all shares, likes, and comments. Total content engagement works as an input for the Engagement Rate, a key metric that is a proxy for the quality of content based on the number of interactions.

Total Digital Audience The total sum of an influencer's potential reach across all his or hers active social platforms, including Facebook, Twitter, Instagram, Pinterest, YouTube, Tumblr, Snapchat, Musical.ly, and Blog monthly unique visits.

Tracking Links URLs that are used to direct traffic to a landing page from somewhere other than your own website. Tracking links are included in marketing campaigns to help brands track, measure, and report the success of an influencer marketing campaign.

Unboxing A specific type of video content that depicts an influencer opening, reacting to, and using various products. It implies a brand sending a package of products while the video shows the influencer unboxing the contents. In a haul video, the influencers have purchased the products themselves and shares the reviews of the items they bought.

User Experience (UX) The overall feeling and experience of a person using a product or a service.

User-Generated Content (UGC) Any form of content created and shared organically by customers or users. An influencer marketing campaign may aim to encourage fans and customers of the brand to share content of the brand.

User Interface (UI) The interactions between the user and the technology of a website, product, or software.

Unique Visitor (UI) The term used to measure the performance of a website that is the number of distinct individuals requesting pages from a website during a given period of time.

Views The number of users who have watched a piece of content.

View-through People who have completed story clip views minus navigation "back" divided by views.

Word of Mouth (WoM) The marketing strategy that relies on satisfied customers sharing opinions and experiences of products and services through oral or written communication with their personal community.

Index

A

Advertising industry, 8
    astronauts, 16
    blockbuster, 10
    consumers, 11
    digital advertising, 8
    eMarketer forecasts, 9
    internet and social media, 15
    media democratization, 12
    meteors, 10
    mobile browser, 8
    pirates, 17
    positive attitudes, 11
    respondents, 9
    traditional advertising, 9
    Walk of Fame, 13
    YouTube impact, 12

App Store traffic creation, 140
    attribution modeling, 140
    developer tracking efforts, 141
    non-tracked majority, 142
    smartphone app, 141
    third-party tracking, 141

Aspirational lifestyle, 2

B

Branded content ads, 144
Budgets, 134–135

C

Changemaker to tastemaker, 1–2
Commodity to valuable asset, 40

Consumer revolution, 4–5
Cream-colored tableware, 2
Creativity, 48
Creator-centric strategies
    brand and campaign
        Adobe, 86
        Museum of Ice Cream, 86
        Revolve Clothing, 86
        Sugar Bear Hair, 85
        YouTube Music, 85
    brand self-assessment, 81, 82
    brands mistake, 81
    community, 83
    consistency, 83
    creativity, 83
    digital and traditional media
        publishing, 89
    expectation, 80
    industry rates, 90
    payment terms set up, 92
    PR strategy, 89
    value beyond pay, 83
    values and personal
        alignment, 87

D

Diffusion of Innovations, 28
    adopter category, 28
    laggards stages., 29
    product adoption, 31

Digital media landscape, 120
    creativity, 132
    definition of success, 123

© Aron Levin 2020
A. Levin, *Influencer Marketing for Brands*,
https://doi.org/10.1007/978-1-4842-5503-2

Digital media landscape (*cont.*)
  marketing campaign types, 123
    action campaigns, 126
    attention campaign, 124
    content campaign, 127
    interest campaign, 125
  marketing objectives and KPIs, 128, 130
  M.A.R.T mnemonic, 123
  primary marketing campaign, 120
    conversion event, 121
    objective and goals, 121
  right campaign strategy, 131
  target audience, 122
  type of content, 133

E

Effective brief to influencers, *see* Influencer
    marketing campaigns
80-20-80-20 strategy, 97
Email communication, 100
  brand collaboration, 108
  budget, 107
  call to action, 115
  capture responses, 114
  create and send email, 111
  creator response, 113
  dynamic model, 107
  email address set up, 100
  import email service provider, 111
  Kill your inbox, 101
  negotiating compensation, 105
  send and receive messages, 103
  skyrockets, 104
  table creation, 109
  third-party software-as-a-service, 102

F, G, H

Framework cheat sheet, 138
Frauds, fake followers and bots, 146
  access to metrics, 148
  audience-first approach, 147
  authentic engagement, 147

I, J, K

Influence, 20
  affinity, 22
  audience size, 21

  formula, 21
  relationship strength, 22
Influencer marketing campaigns
  about brand, 65
  about campaign, 66
  brief template, 65
  goals, 66
  inspiration, 67
  Instagram account @creator, 66
  Pepsi Max, 76
  posts guidelines, 67
  YouTube creator, 68
    creative control, 69
    deliverables, 69
    inclusions, 69
    insight, 68
    objective, 68
    style and messaging, 68
Instagram, 49
  ads content creation, 57
  ambassadorships, 52
  brand experiences, 53
  burst campaigns, 53
  creative strategy scorecard, 58
  fashion and lifestyle verticals, 58
  feed posts and stories, 51
  Hero brand campaigns, 54
  hyper local campaigns, 56
  live for maximum authenticity, 54
  real-time recruitment, 57
  single feed post campaigns, 50
  story-only campaigns, 51
  story polls, 55
  swipe-up lead generation, 56

L, M, N, O

Leaders and followers, 23
  change agent, 27
  diffusion of innovations, 23
  early adopters, 24
  early majority, 25
  innovators, 24
  laggards, 25
  late majority, 25
  product adoption, 24
Longevity of distribution, YouTube, 142
The long tail, 41–46

P, Q

Parameters and values, 137

R

Right influencers, 32
   brand collaboration, 39
   deciding factors, 39
   Instagram categories, 34
   talented and influential content creators, 35
   talent pool strategy, 36
   top-down funnel approach, 36
   YouTube channel categories, 32
Roadblocks, 4

S

Scale relationships, 99

T, U, V

Targets, 136
Theory of constraints, 96–97

W, X

Word of mouth, 69
   AdAge campaigns, 71
   core target segment, 75
   customers mind-blowing, 78

easy-to-talk, 73
exceed expectations, 75
feels good to share, 73
one-size-fits-all solution, 70
Pepsi Max, 76
problem solving, 72
start discussions, 74
SurveyMonkey or Typeform, 77
world is an amazing place, 73

Y, Z

YouTube, 60
Brand/Product Shout-Out, 64
channel categories, 32
Comedy Sketch, 63
favorites, 64
game play, 64
honest opinion, 61
KANOA, 62
longevity of distribution, 142
lookbook, 62
memes, 63
product review video, 61
tutorial/product demo, 61
unboxing videos, 61